A Natural Method Of Physical Training

A NATURAL METHOD
OF PHYSICAL TRAINING

By EDWIN CHECKLEY

—

Cloth, 12mo., $1.50.   Sent post-paid on receipt of price.

—

" Worth its weight in gold."—*New York Herald.*

" His methods and his discoveries are marvelous."
                              —*Dr. Joseph Rhodes Buchanan.*

" Must soon have an army of followers "
                              —*Wm. Blaikie, Author of "How to Get Strong.'*

"This system is the only one that offers a reasonable method of curing obesity."—*Chicago Herald.*

" Its great charm is its simplicity."—*The Critic.*

" A book that every man, woman and child in the world can read with profit."—*St. John (N. B.) Globe.*

" Read this and be strong."—*New York World.*

" Absolutely convincing."—*European Mail.*

"The advice it contains as to the physical training of women and children is timely and admirable."—*Prof. Persifor Frazer.*

" Written by a man who understands his business."
                              —*Medical Review.*

—

WILLIAM C. BRYANT & CO.,

24 AND 26 BROADWAY, BROOKLYN, N. Y.

A NATURAL METHOD

OF

PHYSICAL TRAINING

Making Muscle and Reducing Flesh

Without Dieting or Apparatus

'By EDWIN CHECKLEY

WITH NUMEROUS ILLUSTRATIONS

By H. D. EGGLESTON

New, Revised and Enlarged Edition

BROOKLYN, N. Y.

WILLIAM C. BRYANT & CO.,

1892.

NOTE TO THE REVISED EDITION.

THE immediate success of "A NATURAL METHOD OF PHYSICAL TRAINING" has more than one explanation, but it is doubtless true that the chief cause of the book's popularity has been its effort to present a "natural" method of giving vigor to the body without calling in the artificial aids of apparatus or harsh systems of dieting. Every system of training—the word is used here and elsewhere in the book in its broader meaning and not to signify athletics—that is dependent upon apparatus is necessarily a spasmodic training. Men and women cannot carry such training about with them. If they travel, or are greatly occupied in something that keeps them away from the gymnastic machinery, their training is suspended. The system set forth in this book has attempted to show that the only direct method of keeping the body vigorous is by correcting artificial restraint, carrying the body correctly, breathing correctly and otherwise following a logical system of giving the muscles and organs free and natural play, and opportunity to develop symmetry and strength.

The author has had every reason to be gratified at the indorsements which have been offered by those who have devoted themselves to the science of athletic training, the more as his system radically attacks the older system of college and gymnasium athletics. The author's argument, for instance, that hard muscles are a danger and not an advantage, has begun to receive support from practical and distinguished exponents of the science of muscular development.

The author has been especially gratified at the cordiality of the medical press and profession, which have been all but unanimous in praise of his system as outlined in the present treatise. Here again the indorsement is peculiarily welcome, from the fact that the book might be considered to take an attitude of radical independence toward the medical profession. The truth is that the author has urged his theories in no disrespect to healing science, and is proud to have received such substantial support from physicians of every school. In the last page of the present edition will be found a few of the many comments which have been made by medical journals and practitioners.

A writer may consider himself fortunate when, in a revised and extended edition, he finds himself under no necessity for material modification in any of his chapters. In extending this book the writer has aimed to make some points more clear, and to enlarge in a general way the usefulness of the volume.

PREFACE.

PHYSICAL training is "in the air," but tne observer of current events is able to discover in reports from the athletic world that there is something wrong about most modern methods of training. Muscle-molding schemes that make men die in middle life may be pictorially interesting and may sound heroic, but they are not for that wise average mortal who wishes simply to feel light and strong and, if need be, find himself ready to safely enter on any reasonable physical undertaking. The author of this book believes that there is more "straining" than "training" in a good many popular systems practiced in and out of the college gymnasium, and the method he himself advocates perhaps radically departs from familiar systems. Yet this method seems to the author so fully indorsed by nature and by results that he might, if not for the appearance of egotism, have called this book " *The* Natural

Method of Physical Training," instead of using the indefinite "*A*." In the pages that follow an effort has been made to outline a plan of conduct for bodily development that is not dependent on any appliances whatever, that will build up the frame of the slender and reduce the unwelcome proportions of the corpulent without the employment of machinery or harsh and weakening methods of dieting.

The author fears that he may not always have been able to connect in each chapter all that he had to say upon each point covered, and thus feels that those who wish to follow the system from these pages should carefully read the whole book, observing the emphasis upon seemingly minor matters. E. C.

CONTENTS.

		PAGE
I.	THE BUGBEAR OF TRAINING. . . .	7
II.	HOW TO CARRY THE BODY.	17
III.	HOW TO BREATHE.	31
IV.	MUSCLES AND WHAT THEY DO. . . .	45
V.	THE JOINTS AND THEIR DEVELOPMENT. .	57
VI.	EXERCISES FOR MUSCLES AND JOINTS. . .	71
VII.	THE TREATMENT OF OBESITY. . . .	85
VIII.	TRAINING FOR WOMEN.	101
IX.	A WORD ABOUT CHILDREN.	113
X.	SOME GENERAL HINTS.	123

The Checkley System.

IIIIIIIIIIIIIIIIIIIIIIIIIIIIII

I.

THE BUGBEAR OF TRAINING.

THERE are two points which writers and talkers about physical training are almost always ready to bring forward when discussion arises as to the present status of our race—they tell us to look at the ancient Greeks and at the animal kingdom. They tell us the ancient Greeks attained certain proficiencies in the field of athletics, and developed a remarkably perfect physique, which the artists delighted to reproduce. They show us the muscular perfection of brute creatures, their general health and comfortable relations with life.

These points are in the main well raised. The example of the Greeks was in all respects one toward which the attention of modern peoples may always profitably be turned. The Panhellenic games were an inspiration to the rising generation. They made physical vigor fashionable. And they were not merely an isolated incident in the life of the Greeks. These Panhellenic games were simply the flowering of a superb system of training—superb so far as it related to the work to be done in those tremendous conflicts of the arena. Physicians and law makers alike realized the importance of athletic exercise. Lycurgus scattered free training schools, and his successors followed up, in one way or another, the example set by this remarkable governor. The people paid extraordinary honor to the athletic heroes. A man who won more than one prize at the same Olympiad was modeled in marble by the best sculptor of his state. We are reminded of our own times in the accounts which tell of the large fortunes made by those who achieved some especial glory at the games.

But the conditions of life among the ancient Greeks were wholly different from the conditions of life with which modern men and women are struggling. The athleticism of the old Grecian race was cultivated under very favorable circumstances. The Grecians not only led a more outdoor life than our northern races, but their mode of living, in respect to public and private festivals, entertaiments and social movements, made the development of the physical man much easier than it can ever be with us. These differences do not make it less proper for us to look to the Greeks, but we should remember the necessities arising out of these differences. It is for us to study out the compromise which must be made. Properly made, this compromise will represent a new and sufficient ideal.

It will pay to remember that there has been a good deal of exaggeration in stories of Greek prowess. Undoubtedly we are in possession of some fairly accurate figures concerning the feats of the old athletes, but there are many absurdly false estimates of the early running, jumping and throwing. The Panhellenic games brought forward men who had been in training for great periods for special feats. The honors awarded were so great that no amount of train-

ing and exertion were considered too considerable. Given the same training our modern
athletes would greatly surpass the Greek rec-
ords. If the modern horse is quicker than the
ancient, the modern man is quicker also. Our
all-round athletes would, I am sure, have as-
tonished an audience at an Olmypiad. And as
for the matter of physique, there has been equally great exaggeration on that side. Plato tells
us that the sculptors took considerable liberty
in departing from the actual form of the model.
Everything points to a relative inferiority in
the ancient races; yes, even in the worshiped
Greeks. No one should doubt that the world
is producing men of finer form than it has
hitherto produced, and that it will continue to
do so.

If we consider the other allusion to the
brute creation we shall find many things to
rebuke and instruct us, but many things also
that indicate the possibility of exaggerating the
relative physical superiority of the beasts. Man
is physically the most magnificent of all animals. His muscular system excels in versatility that of any other creature. He can stand

variations in temperature, in forms of covering, in kinds of occupation that are impossible to the lower animals. Considering the things he is in the habit of eating, and the other trials he places upon his system, we can only marvel at the splendid manner in which he is proving his physical superiority to all his other neighbors on this planet.

The significant thing in connection with brute creatures is that they do not have athletics. The lion keeps his marvelous strength without extraordinary effort. And so with other beasts. Their natural habits keep them in condition, and sometimes their natural habits do not seem to fully explain why they are so strong and so healthy. As a matter of fact, beasts are not, of course, always so strong as they would be under training, but by not training they escape other difficulties, of which I will speak a little later on. If we are to take any special lesson from the lower animals, it must be that the best strength is that produced under natural habits.

This brings me to that bugbear of "training." To a certain number of people athletic or special physical training is agreeable. In fact, few who enter it find any kind of training without some exhilaration. But the proportion of people who do any training at all is very small, while the number who might, if the proposed training did not come in the guise of hardship, is unquestionably considerable. The course of exercises prescribed to many an ambitious victim of physical weakness is altogether too heroic, and even those who are fairly strong, and who would like to develop and maintain their strength, are frightened off by the systems put forward as necessary. Elaborate apparatus is one of the symptoms of an elaborate system. The little fellow who went a-fishing was certain he could catch bigger fish the further he went away from home, and the designers of health lifts and chest expanders, boxing machines and rowing appliances seem to feel that the glitter and elaboration of their machinery will tempt and benefit the purchaser in proportion to their size—and complexity.

It is undoubtedly a fact that certain artistic formulas for training have a fascination at the outset. Their ingenuity seems to promise an opening of the mysterious roaᴏ to health. The novelty itself is something to count upon. And machinery has a certain charm while it is new. You pull this and push that so many times a day and you get to be a little amateur Samson. You already feel the muscles expanding. Those biceps especially draw attention, as if they were the synonym of health and strength. But the mystery vanishes after a while and something or other is always interfering with that half hour at the machine. It is put off for a day, for two days, for a week. Interest gradually evaporates and the biceps are allowed to go to the bad again. The illusion disappears and is gone.

And then the corpulent subject is attacked with that terrible legend—"Diet." Leave off eating so and so, is the order, and your paunch will gradually and beautifully disappear. The so and so, of course, is always exactly what the corpulent subject most enjoys. But the worst of it all is that, in spite of obedience, after a terrible struggle, to the awful ordeal, after the discomfort and weakness of implicit reliance on a certain system of eating, there is only a loss.

of a few pounds out of many and no material change in the general form or condition. At the first halt in the rigid dietary discipline there is complete relapse in flesh.

These ordeals bring "training" into very bad repute. Sometimes they do actual injury. The youth who enters the gymnasium at college, starts out on a career of violent training—general as well as special—finds himself exhilarated for a time. His special strength increases, but his false start on the great material lines tells against him in after years, when a little weakness around the heart and a sudden lightness in the head tell a story of bad beginnings and false discipline.

There is something radically wrong in these harsh and extravagant methods of training. The average man does not care to be an athlete in the accepted sense. If he has means to squander in appliances he does not have the opportunity to use them as directed, and the most slavish adherence to the rules somehow does not have the expected effect. The lifting and striking power may be gradually increased and the chest expansion slightly improved, so far as measurement goes, but there is something wanting. Anything that interferes with the galley-slave labor at the apparatus sets back work. The strength of the man so " trained " has no reliance on itself. It is superficial—only skin deep, as it were. The training will not " stay put."

The truth is that there can be no proper training that does not educate the whole system of the man. The muscular system of a man is not made up of chest and biceps. It is a wonderful and complex organization in which one part is intimately related with the other, and if the system as a whole is not kept in mind the building up of the arms will not increase the permanent strength or permanent health. Men become proficient at punching a sand bag who do not know how to simply carry their own body. They have spent their time in training, as it were, from the outside. One of our modern philosophers has said that we invent fine railroads, but we are forgetting how to walk. This is very true. We are forgetting how to stand, and, above all—fatal error !—we are forgetting how to breathe.

There are what are known as "conversa-
tional methods" of learning languages. I sup-
pose these are very good methods. They are
supposed to lead the student into a language
without first learning the grammatical rules.
In athletic training of the simplest kind there
can be no profitable way of skulking around the
first principles. We must breathe properly or
forfeit all chance of ever becoming really strong,
of having the kind of strength that wears well.
We must stand properly if we wish to give the
body and its muscles a chance to become what
we wish them to become and what they must
become to be at their best. The kind of training that starts in to load certain parts of the
body with hard muscles, overlooking the simple
elements of general strength, is an error that
sometimes proves more than a harmless mistake.

In the chapters which follow I shall try,
without elaboration, to outline the general
principles of the muscular machinery and my
system of developing that machinery into comfortable and healthful perfection.

II.

HOW TO CARRY THE BODY.

DOES it, then, need to be told how the body must be carried? Most certainly. It might be asked, Does a person not naturally carry his body as comfortably as he can? And the answer is that a person very seldom does. It may appear that this is being done, but the fact is not so. Some people naturally develop a habit of proper carriage, but they form a decided minority. Without guidance the chances are that a child will grow up into bad habits of holding himself together. His spine will be left to do things it was never intended to do. He will sit, stand and walk without proper reliance on muscles that were intended to make all his movements easier. He will collapse while sitting, rest on his heels, perhaps, while standing, and breathe so perversely that any unusual exertion reveals the fact that only a limited series of muscles are brought into play, while the lungs are but half developed.

It is of the utmost importance, then, at the very outset that a person should do those things properly which occupy so large a percentage of the habits of his life. If there is a reflex action from correct habits of sitting, standing and breathing, to say nothing of other actions, it is quite clear that the formation of a correct habit will bring a certain percentage of added strength and health with no conscious exertion. It is like having money out at interest. The income does not seem to be worked for.

In fact, it is stating a simple truth to say that a man or woman should get good health and sufficient strength and perfection of form in the ordinary activities of life, if those activities, however meagre, are carried on in obedience to right laws. This truth is one of far-reaching yet unsuspected importance. There is a prevailing impression that this, that and the other mode of life prevent the development of a strong body, a superstition that one can-

not be strong without athletics, and violent
athletics at that.   Men carelessly retard and in-
jure their physical system during, say, fourteen
and a half of their waking hours, and then hope
to counteract all this by fifteen minutes' work on
a few muscles of their body, and generally not
on the muscles that are most injured by the
carelessness of the day.

It is a fact not very often taken into account
that *clothes*, in their modern form, have a serious tendency to interfere with the right development of the body, to hinder muscular action
and to generally hamper the physical system.
I do not speak now of such special features as
the corset, but of clothing in general.   Unless
the tendency is specifically checked, most
wearers of fashionable attire will find themselves yielding to the tailor's or dressmaker's
measurements.   The stiff high collar worn by
so many men rather helps the general poise of
the head but is a dangerous obstacle to the
healthy development of the neck muscles.   The
shoulders are, perhaps, particularly influenced by
modern clothes.   A man with low, sloping shoulders holds himself in a position to keep his sus-

penders from slipping, and accommodates himself to the habit of his coat.   Then the conven-
tional "cut" of trousers interferes with easy sitting, walking and stooping.   Men sit so as not to
"bag" or wrinkle their trousers, just as women,
during the reign of the bustle, sat in a lop-sided
fashion to accommodate the mysterious and
ugly appendage.   In many other ways people
of both sexes, and scarcely oftener in one sex
than in the other, are allowing their physical
stature and habits to be strongly influenced by
clothes.

Instead of so doing it is a duty to carry the
body correctly, to move and act in every particular with reference to the health and beauty
of the body without thinking of its covering.
If the covering interferes either ignore the in-
terference or select the covering differently.
Let the clothes fit and protect the body, and
not allow the body to seek the favor of the
clothes.   I have said nothing of shoes, whose
wretched form so often weakens the body by
discouraging exercise and by impairing the
circulation.   Small and ill-fitting shoes have
done as much damage in the world as corsets.

They have made cheerful people peevish and strong people indolent, if not weak. Have shoes large enough to give your feet abundant freedom.

To get out of the ordinary activities of life all possible strength and health let us first learn to *stand*. A literal drawing of the actual standing position of twelve persons chosen at random would present a curious spectacle. The distended abdomen and more or less flattened chest would prevail in a majority of the dozen. It would be safe to say that in eleven out of the twelve the bone structure of the body and not the muscles would be found doing most of the work of keeping the body upright. The incorrect position, more or less characteristic of a great many people, and not by any means representing an extreme case, is shown in the accompanying illustration. The abdomen is here pushed forward into disagreeable prominence, or rather the body is allowed to settle on the legs as it may, thus rounding the shoulders and protruding the abdominal region.

This attitude is just as common among women as among men, and perhaps more com-

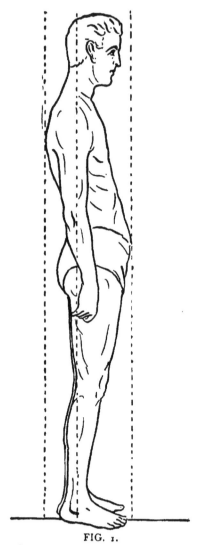

FIG. 1.

Incorrect standing position, very commonly observed among both men and women.

mon. For one thing, corsets, while theoret-
ically holding the body up, encourage lassitude
of the waist region. And then women are
liable to affect a " willowy " style of standing
and moving. Many girls seem to think that
there is a kind of feminine charm in a lacka-
daisical manner.

Now the fact is that the bone structure of
the body should not be forced to perform the
work thus thrust upon it. The muscles should
hold the body in position. Upon them de-
volves the task of holding the trunk erect, of
keeping the proper relation between the spine
and the pelvis (the bone structure from which
the backbone springs) and the upper leg bones
where they join the pelvis, forming what is
called the hip joint. It is worth remembering
that the height of a man may be materially af-
fected by the manner in which he carries his
body. If he uses the muscles of the hip and
abdominal region and of the back instead of
allowing his trunk to settle down, he may be
certain of establishing a better height than if
he did otherwise, and this height will be permanent.

The spine may be relied upon to give a certain support to the trunk. This may go without stating, but the multitude of muscles associated with the spine are intended to perform the greater part of the work in keeping the body in position. As the rudder guides a boat or reins lead a horse, so the muscles direct the posture of the body. They not only direct but largely support the body, and this should be remembered in standing and in every other position and action.

The correct position in standing is sometimes curiously exaggerated by the protrusion of the chest to a grotesque and unnatural degree. Figure 2 may be taken as an example of the position sometimes seriously recommended. There is no naturalness, force or beauty in such a position. The author's views of the correct position are indicated by Fig. 3. As will be seen by this illustration, the lips, chin, chest and toes should come upon one line, with the feet turned at an angle of sixty degrees. In such a position the body acquires its greatest ease, its greatest endurance and its greatest readiness. The chest, the wall covering the great boilers

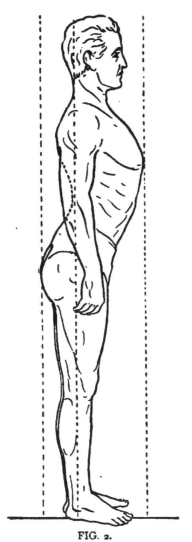

FIG. 2.

Exaggerated standing position, dis-
torting spine and chest.

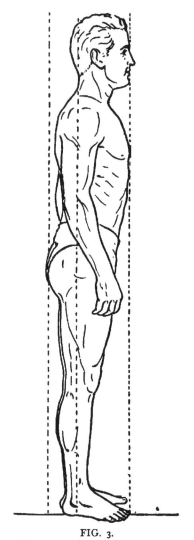

FIG. 3.

Correct standing position, showing
natural and forcible carriage of the
body.

of the body—the lungs—is given the greatest
prominence, while the abdomen is carried more
modestly than most people are inclined to carry
it.   The shoulder, hip and ankle joints are also
kept upon one line.   The neck is carried erect so
as to bring the collar-bone into a horizontal
position.   Notice the difference in the carriage
of the head between Figures 1 and 3.

The point of what I have urged is this:
The muscles must be used in the support of
the body—and all of the muscles that rightfully
should.   This does not imply greater labor, but
less.   What begins by a conscious effort will soon
end in a habit—will become an exhilaration.
What often passes for fatigue of the muscles is
simply irritation arising from impeded circulation of the blood brought about not by the use
but the cramping or non-use of muscles.

This numbness or irritation from impeded
circulation is particularly liable to result from
bad habits in sitting.   In sitting, as in standing, the muscles must be brought into play,
and precisely in proportion to the extent in
which they are used will be the absence of
fatigue in sitting.   It is not to be maintained,

of course, that a person should continually sit bolt upright. This would, for a person compelled to sit during a great many hours each day, entail great fatigue. Some of the muscles may be relaxed and the position modified for short periods, but the muscles should never be so relaxed as to drop the trunk upon the spine, leaving its own bone structure to hold it up. Those who have dropped into this round-backed position will testify to a peculiar weariness in the lumbar region of the spine, what is called the "small of the back." To rise or sit upright and stretch the arms and body affords a great relief. This is not because the muscles have been tired, but because they have been benumbed by failure in the circulation. A proper maintenance of muscular action will keep up the healthy circulation and make it easier to sit for a considerable time without fatigue.

The cultivation of the muscles in the region of the abdomen and the lower part of the back will naturally have the effect of making it easier to sit, as every gain in the strength and extent of a system of muscles builds up a power of involuntary action. In relaxing the trunk the well-drilled army of muscles will be found to have acquired a power to hold the body up with little perceptible effort.

In walking, keep face and chest well over the advanced foot, and preserve the habit of lifting the body with the muscles and by the inflation of the lungs. Of this I shall speak further in connection with the subject of breathing. Avoid a mincing step. Take a free, firm and easy stride, avoiding any hard jarring motions, keeping in mind during every movement or exertion the function of the muscles to support and move the body.

I say "keeping in mind" because I believe that the mind should not be above co-operation with the body. In fact, unless it does co-operate with the body the body cannot be strong and healthy, and if the body is not strong and healthy what can the mind expect to be? In recent years it has become something of a habit with a good many well-meaning people to say high sounding things about the superiority of the mind over the body, the essential insignificance of the body, etc. Is it not time to emphasize the influence of the body upon the mind? Are we not constantly confronted by instances of the mind's dependence upon the body?

What I would like to emphasize is that the mind and body are dependent upon each other. The mind cannot get out of the partnership, however much it may wish to do so. It must stay, and it must do its share or suffer, and generally suffer keenly. The further our civilization advances the more complete this interdependence becomes. Under our fashion of living the body seems to require greater and greater attention from the mind, and the increasing mental strain assumed under our restless, hurrying life makes a greater and greater demand upon the vitality of the body. It is quite clear, then, that we are not in a position to talk about breaking the partnership.

Of course this conscious use of the muscles will not continue to be as great as at the outset. In time the proper management of the body becomes largely unconscious and involuntary, but need never become wholly so.

III.

HOW TO BREATHE.

AT the time of this writing the newspapers contain comments on the illness and death of certain prominent athletes. The winner of many prizes passes away at the age of twenty-four. Lung weakness seizes upon other seemingly stalwart types of "trained" men. These are startling facts. They form a significant comment on some modern methods of drilling the machinery of the human body. If men are to gain muscle at the expense of their life, it is plain that people will soon begin to look askance at training methods of every kind. What is the difficulty? Why has training become dangerous? Why do lung and heart troubles assail in after years the enthusiastic followers of highly active sport?

The answer seems to me to be this: That

modern "training" has become a "straining"
system that is frequently not only indiscreet
but dangerous. It is dangerous not only because of its useless violence and hardship, but
because of the pernicious theories upon which
it is founded. It begins on the outside instead
of the inside. Greater than all its other evils
is its neglect of the lungs.

When we stop for a moment to consider the
tremendous importance of the lungs it must
become apparent that any neglect of these
great central boilers of the body is the worst
kind of neglect. The office of the lungs is of
the very highest importance. This importance
is incidentally acknowledged by many writers
and teachers, but the development of the lungs
is left to take care of itself, it being assumed as
a general thing that all exercises tend sufficiently to expand the lungs. To be sure, great
stress is occasionally laid upon the expansion
of the chest, but the assumption too frequently
appears to be that this expansion is a matter of
external muscular development. The theory
is on a par with the general superficiality of the
average system of training. The strength of

special parts in a steam engine, and even of bands on the boiler, will not prevent weakness and possibly an explosion if the material of the boiler itself is without strength. Hard layers of muscles on the chest do not improve the permanent strength of the lungs.

It should be clear that the enlarging and strengthening of the lungs can be satisfactorily accomplished only by the exercise and special training of those organs themselves—in other words, beginning on the inside. This truth lies at the very bottom of natural physical training.

To learn to breathe is to learn the A B C of physical health, and it is of special importance that this education of the lungs should precede the education of the outer muscular system, for the natural increase of lung strength and chest room is retarded by methods that begin work on the outside first.

What I have to say on this point will become clearer by consultation of Fig. 4, which shows the manner in which the rib system incloses the chest. It will be seen that there is a joint in the ribs as they approach the centre of the chest. From this joint forward to the central strip of bone substance, called the *sternum*, the ribs are made of a flexible cartilage that is readily developed under exercise. Breathing distends the ribs and cartilage in the most effective way; indeed, in the only effectual way. To distend the chest by hollowing the back and throwing back the shoulders is merely a makeshift, while breathing creates a genuine tendency to expansion. The dotted line will indicate the manner in which the rib-structure distends under the interior pressure from the full lungs.

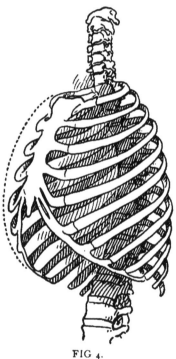

FIG 4.

Showing area of flexible cartilages. Dotted line shows proper direction of expansion.

The general position occupied by the lungs is shown very well in Fig. 5, where they are represented by the shaded parts.

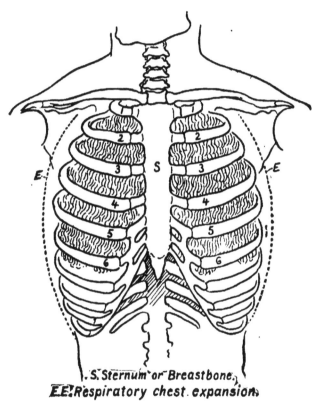

.S. Sternum or Breastbone.
E.E. Respiratory chest expansion

FIG. 5.

The dotted lines on each side again illustrate the chest expansion under full breathing.

It will be noted in Fig. 5 that the lungs do not extend downward beyond the space between the fifth and sixth ribs. This may suggest the reason why the abdomen should not play so prominent a part in breathing as it so generally does. The diaphragm muscle, which separates the region of the lungs from the region of the stomach and liver, has the power to assist the lungs in receiving and expelling the air. But its power has been so greatly abused that the lungs and chest muscles have been left to do very little of the work that properly belongs to them. The unfortunate habit of abdominal breathing, as it is called, is particularly common among men. The use of the corset, and other reasons, have produced among women a habit of breathing with the upper part of the lungs, a habit that has been to that extent fortunate. Lung diseases are less frequent among women than among men. Women breathe less air than men, but they breathe it in a better way. Men generally exercise the lower parts of the lungs nearest the assisting diaphragm, leaving the upper parts, that first receive the air, in a state of relative weakness and susceptibility.

In my opinion the diaphragm has properly no greater necessary use in expanding and contracting the lungs than the ribs themselves. In other words, the action of the diaphragm should be sympathetic without being initiatory. The lungs have their own muscular power, and this power should be fully exercised.

The simplest preparatory exercise is full, long breathing. While standing or sitting in any proper attitude, with the chest free, take in a long breath until the lungs seem full, taking care at the same time not to harshly strain the lungs or muscles. Hold the breath thus taken for a few seconds, and then allow it to slowly leave the lungs. By consciously breathing in this manner the lungs will be enlarged and strengthened and the breathing will become slower. Normal breathing, when the body is at rest, should not include more than ten breaths in a minute. I, myself, get along very comfortably with not more than six, sleeping or waking. During exercise of an ordinary character the breathing will naturally increase to fourteen or fifteen breaths in the minute.

At the outset long breaths will be a conscious exercise. But the reader must not assume that he cannot develop an unconscious habit because the exereise seems at the start to require attention. Take long breaths as often as you think of it. You may not think of it more than once or twice a day at the beginning. Then you will find it easy to remember every hour or so, and then twice or three times an hour, until finally the habit is formed, and the old short, scant breath—a mere gasp in many people—is entirely abandoned. How soon, and to what extent this habit may be formed will depend to a great extent on the constitution of the person, but the principle is of universal application. A long breath will be found to represent strength, and strength that endures. From the elephant, who breathes eight times in a minute, to the mouse who breathes one hundred and twenty times in the same period, brute creatures are almost uniformly found to possess strength in proportion to the length of the respiratory movement. Curiously

enough it is the animal that most closely re-
sembles man—the monkey—who, in confinement, first succumbs to disease of the lungs.

In all lung exercises endeavor to inflate the
lungs upward and outward instead of downward. Carry chest and lungs as if the inflation
were about to lift the body off the ground upward and forward. The feeling of buoyancy
given by this habit is not an illusion by any
means. It is genuine.

There are certain movements which combine
the respiratory with muscular exercises. Such
a preliminary exercise is indicated in Fig. 6.
Take the correct standing position and place
the hands together (locking the thumbs), as
shown in the drawing at A. Raise the hands,
keeping the arms straight, and at the same
time take in a long breath. When the arms
are raised as high as your muscular condition
will allow without bending the body in any
way, slowly lower the arms again, emiting the
breath as they descend. Repeat this a number of times. When the shoulder and chest
muscles are in good condition, you will be able
to raise the arms straight over the head without bending the body.

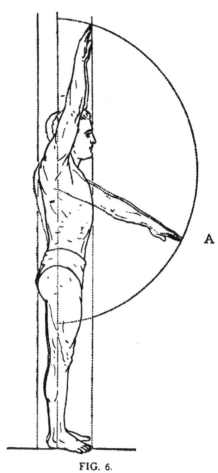

FIG. 6.

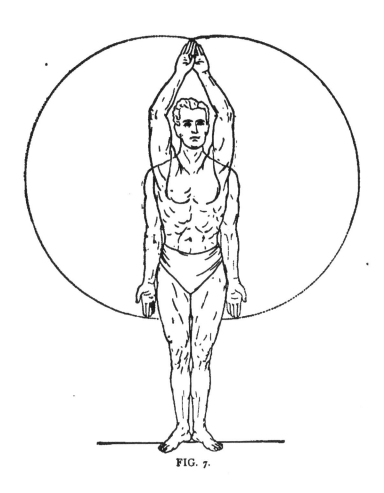

FIG. 7.

For another exercise combining respiration and muscular action assume the same position, raise the hands slowly while taking in a breath, and when they have reached a position over the head hold the breath while they are brought slowly down to the sides. Then slowly release the breath. Again, place the hands over the head as in Fig. 7, and as they are brought to the sides on a perfect line, draw in a breath corresponding in duration to the time occupied in dropping the arms slowly. Release the breath gradually.

For a final exercise in this department the preliminary position is shown in Fig. 8. Having brought the elbows on a level with the shoulders, and the hands on the same line, extend the arms, with hands together as if in the act of swimming, taking in at the same time all the air the lungs will hold. Holding the lungs full, bring the hands around on an outer circle to points on a level with the shoulders, and then slowly empty the lungs while bringing the hands to the original position.

These exercises will be found easy yet exhilarating, and will fill the double office of

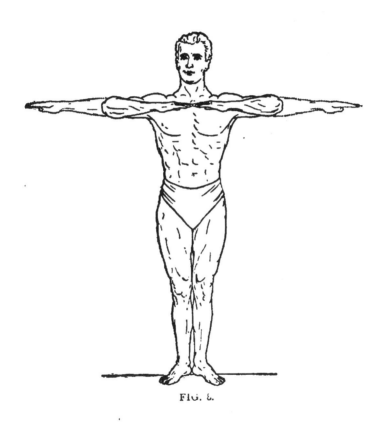

FIG. 8.

strengthening the lungs and developing the shoulder and chest muscles. Practice them after rising and before fully dressing in the morning, and again before retiring at night. It should not be difficult to find some opportunity for this practice some time again during the day. These movements should not be performed more quickly than ten times a minute.

It is well not to overdo these or other exercises at the outset, since, by unduly tiring the muscles, the pleasure of exercising on the ensuing day will be largely destroyed by a sense of pain. Nothing is gained by straining.

IV.

MUSCLES AND WHAT THEY DO.

BEFORE passing to the general training of the muscular system it cannot be inadvisable to pause for a moment and consider what a muscle is and what it is capable of doing. I have more than once seen men, speaking of their power to strike a blow, proudly touch the bunch of muscle on the top of the upper-arm, as if that supplied the power in striking, when, in fact, it is the muscles on the back of the arm that supply the force by which the arm is straightened. Incidents of this kind furnish a reminder that very few people realize the character—the structure—of muscles, or understand clearly the functions they perform. Indeed, judging from the systems of training now so common, and the conduct of athletes in general, it seems questionable whether a knowledge of the muscles, their needs and application, is even as well diffused as many have supposed.

Generally speaking a muscle is formed of a mass of small fibres running parallel with one another, and possessing a power of contraction more or less great, according to their health and training. This power of contraction draws closer to each other the two ends of the muscles, and by so doing brings the bones to which the two ends are attached that much nearer together. The muscle is attached to the bone by white, unelastic cords called tendons. These tendons are so strong and so securely fastened to the bone that the sudden contraction of the muscle in pulling is more liable to snap the bone than the concussion of a fall itself. Muscles, indeed, break a great many bones in one way or another.

The muscles of the body are arranged for the most part in complimentary groups, by which they act together, pulling and relaxing as the case may be. Thus in the limbs the muscles which straighten the bones are called the *extensor* muscles, while those that bend them are called *flexor* muscles. The *biceps*

on the front of the upper arm are *flexor* muscles, because they pull up the fore-arm. To
straighten out the arm again the *triceps* on the
back of the arm exercise their office as *extensors*. In the same manner the *flexors* of the
leg are on the back and the *flexors* of the
hand are on the palm.

The ac-
companying
illustration
(Fig. 9,) will
give an idea
of the manner
in which the
biceps act in
bending the
arm. The ten-

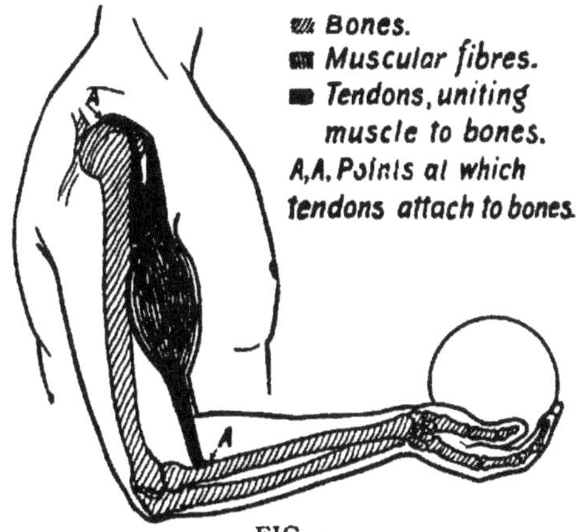

Bones.
Muscular fibres.
*Tendons, uniting
muscle to bones.*
A,A. *Points at which
tendons attach to bones.*

FIG. 9.

don joins the forearm not far below the elbow
joint, thus giving the muscles a very quick
leverage on the arm. With so short a hold,
however, this muscle requires great power.
Of course in flexing the arm, the forearm
muscles—which, in their turn, are united with
the upper arm—are also brought into play.
When the muscles on the front and back of

the arm are both drawn at once the limb becomes rigid. The same remarks apply to Fig. 10, which shows the chief muscles that carry the body on the toe. The bone of the heel forms a sort of lever upon which the contracting muscles in the "calf" of the leg operate.

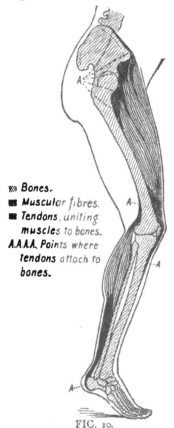

Bones.
Muscular fibres.
Tendons, uniting muscles to bones.
A.A.A.A. Points where tendons attach to bones.

FIG. 10.

In order to feel any of the muscles to the best advantage establish some resistance—such as a weight in the hand to discern the flexors, and a pressure downward against some obstacle to watch the action of the extensors — the muscles on the back of the arm. The function of the muscle is thus to *pull*. Every movement of which the body is possible is brought about by the *pulling* of one or more muscles.   The pulling is, as I have said, accomplished by the contraction of the muscles, and this power of contraction is inherent in them.   It belongs to their very nature; for while our will generally telegraphs through what are called the motor nerves what it wishes the muscle to do, the muscle will contract under certain circumstances without any order from the will.   Indeed, if a muscle is removed from the body it will still contract under stimulus from pinching or from the sting of acid.   Of course it is the duty of every healthy being to keep the muscles as perfectly under the control of the will as possible.   The partnership between the brain and the muscles should be complete and continuous.   It may be set down as an absolute truth that no one will become unconscious of his body in the right sense until he has first become thoroughly and intelligently conscious of every part of it.

Now the contractility of a muscle, the power it has to shorten and draw its ends closer together, depends on the extent and condition of the *fibres*, the bulky part of the muscle as dis-

tinguished from the hard and uncontractable
tendons. These fibres, looking, when highly
magnified, like a bunch of red worms all
stretched in the one direction, form the *meat* of
the body as distinguished from the bone and
gristle. In fact, the muscles make up in weight
more than half the bulk of the body. From
this it may be judged without argument that
the health of this machinery is of very great
importance to the
health of the body.
The muscles are not
implements which may
or may not be used and
cultivated according to
the taste and pursuits
of the person. They must be used and developed or the body will •fall into ill-health.
They are more than half of us and must be
taken into consideration in a serious and intelligent manner.

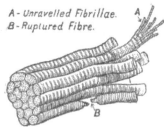

A - Unravelled Fibrillae.
B - Ruptured Fibre.

FIG. 11.

The chief reason why the muscles must be
kept in use is that their health directly effects
the circulation of the blood, and upon the perfect circulation of the blood physical health is

greatly dependent. The moment a muscle is put in action the blood dances through it with increased speed. As it develops, more and more blood is called to supply it. In its greatest heat it is greatly charged with blood. It is for the same reason that *all* of the muscles should be called into play in the general carriage and use of the body, for if the activity of certain muscles quickens and improves the circulation, and the disuse and ill-health of other muscles disturbs the circulation in another part it is quite plain that the general circulation will be at a loss. The result will be coldness in the feet and hands, and a constant danger to the weaker organs of the body. A sluggish circulation, resulting from the disuse of large areas of the muscular system, means many terrors to the unfortunate victim. Neuralgia and kindred complaints are a frequent result of inactivity and confinement. The first step toward a cure of such ills should not be drugs, but studious deep breathing and exercise.

People are frequently astounded by the great strength of an athlete. The trained man, lumpy with muscles and glowing with health, lifts some tremendous weight and carries it for a distance. The feat, incredible to the hearer, is scarcely comprehended even by the spectator. What does it mean? Are the athlete's direct lifting muscles so much beyond the normal in power?

The truth is that the athlete's effort is successful, not so much because his individual muscles are greatly superior to the same muscles in the normally developed man, but because he *uses more of them.* The majority of people do not know half the muscles they own. If they unexpectedly make use of a muscle long left out of account and in a half dead condition, it gives them a twinge, they are frightened off. They rub it with arnica and endeavor never to use it again. They lift, carry, stoop, reach and climb with scarcely a majority of their muscles. Of course, in a violent exercise like some forms of dancing, a large proportion of the muscles are brought into play, but many of them only slightly and only under such exceptional conditions. It is in an understanding of the scope of the muscular action in a given movement that a man will secure power in that movement.

Take the case of a blow with the fist. In a gymnasium a number of young men will gather near a suspended sand bag. One after the other will hammer at the object forcing it to swing at various angles. The owner of perhaps the stoutest arms only sends it out at right angles. Then steps up a young man of comparatively light-weight and triceps inferior in bulk to those of many of the others. This young man strikes a blow at the bag and it bounds clean over the point of suspension. How did he do it?

In the first place the young man knew the right moment in the extension of the muscles at which to make contact with the bag; but particularly he knew how to throw all of his muscles and all of his weight into the blow. He used every muscle he possibly conld, down to the tendon Achilles in his heel, and he made every one do all it possibly could.

The continuous health and use of all the muscles will thus not only have the effect of securing that great boon to the system—a free circulation—but it will give an incalculable advantage in every muscular effort. The body

acquires not only greater power, but greater
ease and grace. It acquires in general the
great sustaining power of distributed responsi-
bility. A man or woman who holds the body
erect, or in any necessary posture, with the aid
of but a few trained muscles, possibly supported
by a few others that are occasionally called
into play and that soon tire, grows fatigued
much sooner than one whose weight is carried
by a well-drilled army of fibres, fully supplied
with stimulating blood.

When it comes to training the muscles, their
relation to the blood circulation should never
be overlooked. That this relation is continually overlooked in modern athletic training I
need scarcely say. It is very well understood
that modern training is too often engaged in
making muscles "hard," as if their mere hardness was a sign of the most valuable condition
To be sure a man covered with hard muscles
will often display great immediate power, but
not of endurance, and of after health he can
have little chance.

The highest state of health and power in a
muscle will always lie in its flexibility rather

than in its hardness. A man trained until his muscles "feel like iron," is really in a dangerous condition. He soon gets out of "training," and is then immediately at a loss. His muscles feed upon his vitality, and, especially when he has passed middle-life, threaten his general health. A man so "muscle bound," as the saying goes, is not in possession of a power. The power owns him.

On the other hand, a man who keeps his muscular system in a state of comparative softness and high flexibility can not only summon great strength, but his powers of endurance are surprising. He is, too, easily kept in training. Natural exercise will preserve his condition, and he is at any time ready to train for special effort, if that is necessary, without shock or inconvenience.

Muscular exercise, however slight, results in a waste of tissue in the flesh fibres, and this waste is carried off. During repose the blood returns new material, and the stimulated action increases the area of blood circulation and enlarges the muscular mass. When exercise is properly conducted this waste and renewal go gradually and easily forward, preserving complete health in the parts and steadily increasing the resources. But when the exercise is unnecessarily violent the destruction of tissue is injuriously carried on. The process of repair cannot so nicely supplement the waste as in the case of reasonable exertion. And when exercise is introduced infrequently — after periods of almost complete inaction—it cannot atone for the sin of collapse. It will not do, as I have suggested, to sit, stand and move badly for ninety-nine one hundredths of the time and then hope to make things come out even by one per cent. of right exercise.

The muscles will have the greatest health, strength and "staying" power that are kept flexible and full of blood by continuous use in every day life. To expect them to keep healthy by an infrequent fifteen minutes at some machinery, is as unreasonable as to think of preserving the comfort of the stomach with one meal a week.

V.

THE JOINTS AND THEIR DEVELOPMENT.

THIS is not a surgical treatise and my desire is to spare the reader or student as much as possible of dry, scientific detail. But the most common-sense view of this training matter, especially if we are to work from the inside, demands that we should constantly keep in mind the structure of the body. We have a certain physical system to work on. That is our foundation, and it will be of no avail to ignore either the limitations or the possibilities of that system.

I have never believed that the creator had this or that *intention* about the body. If the creator had any definite intention about the physical machinery of man, it was that that machinery should be of the utmost service to man, and that it should be made all that its owner can make it. What we really mean when we speak of intention is that the splendid mechanical arrangement of the bones and muscles seems to have an especial adaptability to this or that function. I have already spoken of the beautiful versatility of t h e human physique. Man's bone structure gives him a scope of movement nowhere equaled among the lower animals. This is because man's intelligence has taught him to aid his own development in every useful direction. The horse, for instance, with its short collar bones and undeveloped lateral muscles, has all of his power in forward and backward movements, and almost none in movements to one side or the other. Every one has noticed how difficult it is for a fallen horse to raise himself. The horse has only developed the muscles that are most useful to him in the service of man. Man finds so many uses for his own joints and muscles that he is continually bringing them to a higher state of versatility.

But he by no means uses his bone system as it might and should be used. He gives only a half-use to his joints as he gives only a half-use to most of his muscles. This is very largely because he usually has but a very slight knowledge of the actual location and capacity of his joints. He bends his spine in stooping as if there were no hip joints in his anatomy. It is often remarked that man first ascertained the location of his stomach when an indiscreet meal brought confusion in that locality. Most of us forget about the joints until some novel slip or movement gives the unused machinery a twinge, and then, instead of following up the lesson and making that joint serviceable, we are very liable to avoid any further service in the offending part.

The extremities of two or more bones forming a joint are covered with cartilage, which, as I have said, is a solid but softer substance than bone, and one whose smoothness and elasticity keep the ends of the bone from wearing. As in the case of all other material of the body, this cartilage is in best health when the function it has is evenly and naturally exercised. The cartilage is covered with a thin layer called the *synovial membrane*, and

the joints are continually oiled and kept
in working condition by a fluid called *synovia.*
Then a series of tough bands, called *ligaments,*
hold the heads of the bones in proper position.

Joints like those at the knee and ankle are
called hinge joints, while others, like those at
the shoulder and hip, are ball and socket
joints. One is constructed very differently
from the other but both are operated on the same
principle and have the same general conditions
of health and strength.

The joint itself, if we were to mean the
bones merely, has all the flexibility that the
surrounding ligaments and the connecting
muscles will give it. That the difficulty of
bending is not in the bones but in the ligaments and muscles about the bones will be
illustrated by the fact that one has little difficulty in placing the knee against the chest.
But stand upright and endeavor to carry the
chest toward the knees and the operation is
found to be very difficult. Or endeavor to lift
the stiffened leg toward the chest, and it will
be found impossible to acquire the whole distance. This is because the muscles and ten-

dons have not been trained to sufficiently accommodate themselves to the severe relaxation. When the joints are not fully trained by use the same difficulty will constantly arise, and even in the minor movements.

The ligaments are necessarily made to hold the bones very firmly. If they did not cases of dislocation would be much more frequent than they now are. When a bone becomes dislocated the ligaments and muscles draw the points of union past each other. In the case of the shoulder this is not a very serious affair, for that joint, being relatively in a state of high flexibility, may usually be reset without great difficulty. Many contortionists can voluntarily dislocate one or both of their shoulders by muscular action, and restore their position without difficulty. But in the case of the thigh, for instance, the situation is very different. A visitor to a hospital will often observe a patient lying with one leg extended on a support ending in a pulley and weights. The weights, sometimes of many pounds, are " tiring out " the contracting elements about the joint. When they are sufficiently " tired " by the pro-

longed pulling, and acknowledge themselves
beaten, the head of the dislocated bone is
placed in position and the muscles again acquire the necessary contractility.

It is thus important that in developing the
muscles of the body the office of the joints
should be kept in mind. The bones are not
insensible material but contain a blood system,
a life and sensitiveness equal to that of the
other parts of the body. They are, in fact, as
much dependent upon exercise for health as
the muscles. Moreover, a bone may be increased in dimensions by exercise, so that the
chances of increasing the height and building
out the frame by carrying the body in the best
manner. will be aided by the actual growth of
properly exercised bones.

The proper use of the hip joint is, perhaps,
most frequently ignored. As I have suggested
the bones of the spine are continually strained,
the chest contracted and the abdomen distended
in an effort to save the hip joint and the muscles
affecting its use from performing the service
that belongs to them.

By frequent and easy practice the hips may

be made what they should be—the natural hinge in the middle of the body. Begin by ascertaining with the finger the location of the hip joints. Place the middle finger of each hand on the corresponding hip joint—at the exact locality of the hinge—and the thumbs of each hand on the edge of the hip or pelvis itself. Now bend forward and the relation of the pelvis bone to the leg joint will be readily perceived by the touch of the thumbs and fingers. The action of bending is, indeed, a backward movement of the hinge of the body and not a forward movement of the head as the beginner generally assumes. Let the conscious movement be in the hips, and preserve the natural relations of head, neck and back. Repeat several times the motion of bending from an upright position to a point as low as possible *without bending the back.* At the outset a stick of any sort—a broom handle if you choose—may be held with one hand upright against the spine, head, hollow of the back and foot of spine, all touching, while the stooping over is tried several times, until the straightness of the back is secured, and it becomes plain that the hips

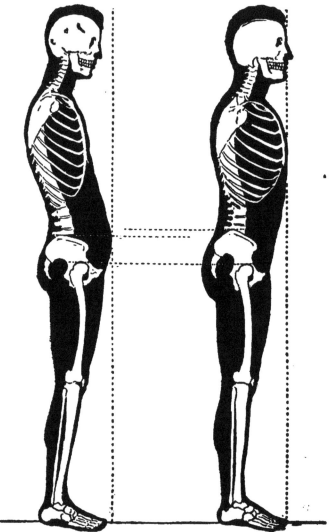

FIG. 12.

Illustrating the bone system of the body as seen in the incorrect and correct standing positions and the manner in which the proper use of the hip (or pelvis) and back muscles may increase the height and symmetry of the body. The figure to the right is that of a man naturally two or three inches shorter than the figure to the left.

are doing all the bending. When the motion i;
first tried the pupil invariably arches the head
and neck, and perhaps hollows the back.

For the purposes of this practice guard
against any movement of the back or neck,
and the value of these fine hip hinges will begin to appear. Repeat these movements with
the hands raised above the head. Then bend
forward as far as the hip joints will allow,
throw the shoulders up and forward, and touch
the floor with the tips of the fingers, without
bending the knees. The latter movement is a
familiar feature of the military "setting up"
drill and is of great value. When first attempted
it is generally found difficult, though some
persons, with no special effort, easily bend in
this way. After repeated practice it will be
found possible not only to touch the floor but
to hold the fingers there, then to touch and
hold the second joint of the fingers and finally,
perhaps, even the palms.

The action of the shoulders in this movement brings up the importance of developing
the shoulders. The power of the shoulder
movement in itself is surprising. Stand up-

right in the correct position and lift the shoulders as high as possible, lowering them afterward as far as they will go. Now bring them forward and draw them back as far as they can reach in each direction. Repeat these movements and endeavor to keep the shoulders flexible and vigorous. By training the shoulders the clavicle, or collar bone, with the other bones and muscles involved, increase the width and general bulk of the shoulders.

A special exercise for the development of the shoulders with the muscles of the back and sides is this : Stand sideways near some vertical surface, like the wall of a room, at a point sufficiently distant to allow the hand when extended to easily touch the surface. Now move an inch further away and touch the surface again without altering the position of the feet, legs or pelvis (Fig. 13.) A second time move an inch and this time there will be some difficulty in reaching. Repeat the movement until the surface cannot be reached, then do the same with the other arm and shoulder. The effort to reach will draw out and straighten the shoulders, and it will be discovered that the shoul-

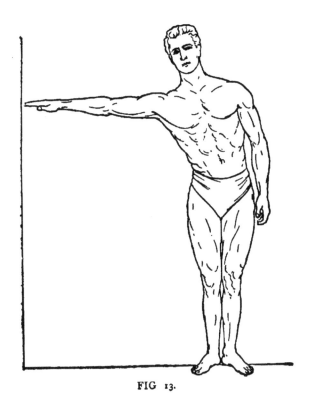

FIG 13.

ders can be made to have a distinct lateral
extension. Stand with the back to the wall
and the arms extended and make a pencil
mark at the ends of the second fingers when
the s h o u l d e r s are most contracted. Now
reach out as far as possible each way, and the
difference in reach will be found, at the end of
a few of the exercises just given, to steadily
increase. After a few months of reasonable
practice with the shoulders the tailor may, if it
has been his practice, be requested to leave out
the cotton padding in the coat.

There is a complimentary action between
the shoulder and hip that is well illustrated in
the act of stooping. An effective method of
stooping is shown in Fig. 14. The first bending is of the knee. Then the hip hinges work
and the body bends forward—partly move the
shoulders, by which the hand is easily brought
to the ground without the wrenching of the
spine and the discomfort of both lungs and
abdomen. In such movements the tendency
is to distend the abdomen, but in this and in
all similar movements the abdomen should be
contracted and kept under muscular control.

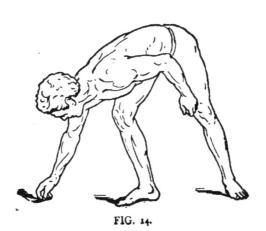

FIG. 14.

In the same manner when seated do not reach over a table, for instance, by curving the back, but by throwing forward the shoulder. If this does not bring the hand near enough the object, bend at the hips. The great value of a flexible shoulder in reaching is shown by the fact that, with the spine firmly held against the back of a chair, the hand may, with practice, be osillated in a direct forward reach from two to six inches.

I have thus far but sketched the value of a proper training for the joints. In another chapter I shall take up a series of exercises bringing both joints and muscles into play.

VI.

EXERCISES FOR MUSCLES AND JOINTS.

ALL exercises of the joints involve certain exercises of the muscles, but there are some that involve simply a relaxation of certain muscles with only sufficient tension in others to keep the body erect meanwhile. Such, for instance, is this useful exercise for the attainment of flexibility in the pelvic region or the region of the hips :

Take the correct standing position, then relax the muscles so as to permit the whole weight of the body to fall on the left leg, allowing the right leg to bend and the right hip to sag down as far as it may. Now transfer this weight to the right leg and allow the left hip to drop as loosely as possible. This would be a very bad position to stand in, but the exercise of transfering the weight from one side of the pelvis to the other, gives increased flexibility and vigor to the muscles and ligaments of this region, and will give increased elasticity and endurance in walking. On the first occasion the exercise should be repeated slowly, and might last one or two minutes. After renewed practice it will be found easy to drop rapidly from one hip to the other without inconvenience and to prolong the exercise for four or five minutes.

The training of the spine should be carried on with the training of the pelvis, from which bony framework it rises. In pointing out that the spine should not be bent in every stooping and reaching movement, the theory was not that it was to its disadvantage to bend, but that the habit of bending forward needlessly hampered the lungs and digestive region. The spine itself should be thoroughly exercised, for the same reason that other regions should be kept in reasonable activity.

To give the spine a flexibility necessary to the comfort of the body it should be frequently moved in all directions consistent with its structure. Under proper cultivation the spine has great versatility of movement. Between each of the bones of the spinal column are disks of "fibro-cartilage," as the anatomists call it, a substance which operates as a cushion between each section of vertebræ and constituting a continuous safeguard against accident to the great bone centre of the body. These cushions form actually about one-fourth of the spinal column, and they not only render the column susceptible of modification, so far as its lengthening or shortening is concerned, but they make it possible for the column to twist vertically to a considerable extent. Numerous ligaments, forming a beautifully complex structure, hold the whole system of bones and cushions in position, and the stout muscles of the back hold an intimate relation with them. It is these ligaments and muscles that require to be treated in the exercise of the spine.

An exercise of a simple but effective character is acquired in this way: After assuming the correct standing position, extend the arms until the hands are brought on a level with the shoulders. Holding the arms and shoulders

upon a straight line and keeping the arms
directly opposite each other, as if actually held
in position by a long pole passed across the
baek of the neck and held in position by the
thumbs (this plan may be followed if desired),
swing the arms and shoulders in unison, first in
one direction and then in the other until the
line of the arms, at the extreme tension of the
swing, is as nearly as possible at right-angles
with the first position. Swing in this way at
the rate of about twenty movements to the
minute until the muscles of the shoulders and
back feel tired. The greatest flexibility will be
found in the upper region of the spine—a slight
flexing of each section of the vertebræ, giving
an aggregate twist that will, with practice, become considerable. If the arms do not swing
the shoulders with them, the exercise will have
little value. And it is to be remembered that
the hips should, during the exercise, keep
their natural position and not swing with the
shoulders.

A variation upon this exercise is illustrated
in Figs. 15 and 16. In Fig. 15 the arms are
brought to a position at right-angles with their

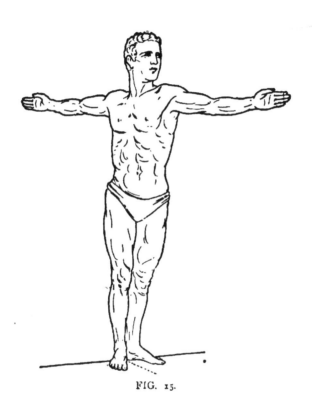

FIG. 15.

FIG. 16.

original line, the hips in this case being turned slightly. Now, keeping the arms rigidly opposite each other, bend the left arm downward, at the same time bending the left knee only, and touch the floor between the two feet, as shown in Fig. 16. Raise the left hand until the arms resume the position of Fig. 15, and swing the arms about until the right hand occupies a forward position. Bending the right knee (the left being kept rigid), the floor may now be touched in the same manner with the right hand. These positions may be alternated at the rate of about fifteen changes to the minute. The exercise is an excellent one.

In the two movements just described keep the face directed toward one point in front of the figure. By so doing the neck will be given some work to do and will be strengthened in all repetitions of the exercise. To further strengthen the neck—and a development of the neck muscles will prevent many a headache that arises from no other cause but muscular fatigue—stand with the back against a wall. Without moving any part of the back or shoulders away from the wall, move the head for--

ward and back a number of times, keeping the
face on the same vertical line as when the back
of the head touches the wall. Then practice
a side to side movement of the head, *without
altering the vertical line of the head*, as in Fig.
17. In this second movement it will be found
very difficult at the beginning not to roll the

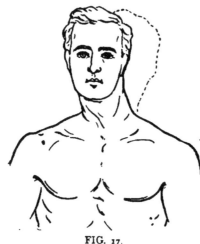

head, but be content
with a slight move-
ment at the outset,
and in time it will
be found possible to
oscillate the head
several inches with-
out altering the ver-
tical line.

The great ad-
vantage of move-

FIG. 17.

ments of the neck, in which the head is managed
independently, is an increased control of all the
muscles in this region of the body. It is thus not
merely the *exercise* of the muscles that all these
movements are designed to accomplish, but
the *control* of the muscles, so that every muscle
may, in so far as that is possible in ordinary

training, be under reasonable control. The value of such perfection of control 1 cannot reiterate too frequently. The exhilaration, the increased iocal strength, and the increased general health, are certain to render control worth the effort.

An exercise of much value in perfecting the poise and supleness of the body, and in strengthening the legs, is illustrated in Fig. 18. Assume the standing position, with the hands at the sides. Draw the arms backward until the hands are about eighteen inches from the vertical line of the body, relax the leg muscles and drop quickly into the position shown in the drawing. As the body descends, bring forward the hands, and by continuing their swing the balance of the body will be better preserved while it sinks and rises again to the first position. The natural elasticity of the muscles will tend to send the body upward again after it has dropped upon the heels, and the movement may be repeated, according to the condition of the muscles, from three or four to a dozen times. Remember to keep the body above the hips perfectly upright during the exercise.

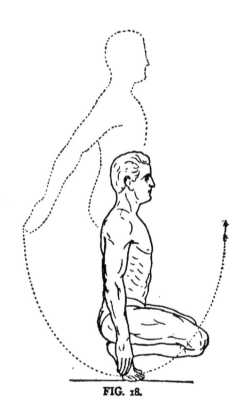

FIG. 18.

Another exercise, benefiting the legs, hips and chest: Place one foot before the other as in stepping, rise on the toes (or, properly speaking, the ball of the foot), and springing slightly transpose the relative positions of the feet so that by a regular repetition the effect will be as of a still walk. The arms may be swung in sympathy with the movement. During the exercise practice a long and steady breathing —with the lips closed, of course.

It will he observed that while some of these exercises place considerable tax on the agility of the muscles, there are none of them violent. Dozens of other movements pursuing the same line of development will readily occur to one who enters upon practice. My purpose is always to lead the pupil by gradual steps to the point where he or she shall feel a perfect familiarity with and mastery of all the muscles of the body. When this has been accomplished, in connection with the development of the lungs, the pupil is ready for the heavier athletic training, with which this book is not concerned, and with which all but a small number of people have neither the time nor the necessity to be interested.

Even sedentary people will find many ways of amplifying in practical exercise the foregoing special exercises for the lungs, muscles and joints. Yet it is necessary to avoid violent experiments. In lifting anything whatever, endeavor to bring all the necessary muscles into play. The action will require a certain amount of thought, for in a spasmodic effort it is easy to seriously strain a few muscles left to do an involuntary service. In fact, a failure to concentrate effort in the right manner often does an injury, when the movement intelligently made exhilarates without straining or "winding" the person.

In his recent scientific work on the "Physiology of Bodily Exercise," Dr. Lagrange emphasizes this point : "Exercise," says the writer, "performed without moderation or rule induces all forms and degrees of fatigue, and exposes the human machine to various injuries which we have described as the accidents of work. On the other hand, muscular work performed in gradually increasing quantity and according to the rules of graduated training, bring about a progressive adaptation of the organs in the performance of more and more violent exercise. It improves t h e human motor by giving to all its machinery a greater strength and ease of working. Such are the results of exercise considered as an abstract factor and reduced to the *quantity* of work represented by it. But it is only by a mental effort that we can isolate the work done by the system from the organs concerned in the performance. Now these organs are not the same in all cases, and do not work in the same manner in all forms of exercise. Thus, the practice of different exercises produces different effects on the system. Hence the use of a rational classification of the different exercises, and the necessity of making a choice from among them in accordance with the effects desired."

Light exercises and exercises that vigorously tax the strength each have their place and value. The point is that they should not be misplaced. The exercises given are designed to *awaken* the muscular system, to give it flexibility and readiness, and it will be found when the training on these lines has been carefully advanced, that a heavy demand on the muscles has no terrors, that the general strength has been splendidly increased in a degree entirely out of proportion to the increased size of the individual muscles.

VII.

THE TREATMENT OF OBESITY.

"LET me have men about me that are fat," says the Cæsar of Shakespeare's play. But then there may be too much of a good thing. There is a happy mein between the "lean and hungry" proportions of Cassius and the too ample outlines of the Leicester gentleman who, early in this century, carried to his grave a body weighing 789 pounds. In our own day, with all the hurrying and scurrying brought by the Nineteenth Century method of living, a large number of people suffer from an accumulation of fat, and the treatment of persons so afflicted receives much attention and calls up many ingenious schemes and suggestions.

The most popular method of combating corpulency is by dieting. A thousand and one pamphlets and patent medicines bear promises of salvation for the afflicted fat. Many a worthy person has suffered the agonies of semi-starvation in an effort to reduce his weight, and has sometimes succeeded in getting rid of a few pounds. Many others have chosen to "eat and drink" if they cannot "live and be merry," preferring the inconveniences and dangers of corpulency to the tortures of a greatly restricted diet.

So long as certain articles of food are recognized as having greater properties for producing fat than others, it is plain that dieting may have some influence on the quantity of fat accumulated. But it only succeeds in reducing the formation of fat, and does nothing toward getting rid of fat after it is formed. In a person otherwise healthy this can only be done by exercise—not merely abstract "airings," which fleshy people sometimes consider exercise, but locally applied exercise, intelligently and conscientiously pursued.

Regarded rightly obesity is simply a disease and must be specifically treated like any other disease. When the natural functions of the body proceed without interruption there can be no accumulation of fat. It is only by the failure of some natural process that fat increases beyond the desirable point.

In the growth of the body-materials fat is accumulated and consumed again just as steadily as coal is burned in the engine, or as the chemical ingredients of an electric battery are gradually exhausted. This fat feeds the muscles—every muscular effort producing a certain amount of combustion. If the muscles are not exercised, the fatty substance, which would be burned up and carried off by the action of the muscles, steadily accumulates.

The accumulation of fat under the absence of exercise operates against its owner in more ways than one. Not only does it increase his weight, retard his movements by increasing bulk, and interfere with his breathing, but it unduly heats the body. The blood of a fat person is likely to become overheated, and is difficult to cool. Thus these excessive layers of fat, operating like so many excessive layers of clothing, are a constant menace to the comfort and the health of the body.

Exercise directly attacks superfluous fat. How much fat may be superfluous depends upon the constitution and temperament of the person. Under the most vigorous training some people retain a good deal of fat. They are by nature plump. But their fat is no detriment to them. They move with as much ease and as little breathlessness as other people. The quantity of fat to be lost under exercise thus depends upon the individual, but will always, of course, be considerable in proportion to the amount accumulated without exercise and under the unrestricted influence of the disease at its height.

Exercise not only reduces fat but it reduces it in the most direct and effective way. In half an hour of vigorous exercise a man may reduce his weight by a pound or more. The rapidity with which fat may be burned off in the activity of the muscles is often, indeed, surprising. This dissipation of fat is local; that is to say, it disappears in localities in which muscles are active, and in proportion to their activity. Thus people will accumulate fat in accordance very largely with their personal habits. People who sit a great deal, yet have occasion to use their arms considerably, will be found with arms having proportionately more muscle and less fat than their legs. Others who are on their feet a great deal, but take little exercise, are often found with relatively slender and muscular legs, while body and arms are very fleshy.

A large number of people, while of seemly proportions in other respects, grow an abdomen that is exceedingly ugly and becomes in time a great inconvenience. This is because, while the general activity of the person is considerable, their abdomen is kept free from muscular action. The worship of the stomach renders people who like to live well extremely jealous of anything that disturbs the region of the stomach and digestive organs. Perhaps eating excessively renders them continually cautious about bending, and at the first signs of a protruding abdomen in a person otherwise slender the protrusion is patted and petted as a kind of symbol of health, when, in fact, it is sometimes, if not very often, a threatening sign. It is at least a prophecy of too much fat, and as such should be looked at askance.

Instead of coddling the abdominal region it
is a duty to keep this region as much alive with
good muscles as any other part of the body.
Where muscles are healthy excessive fat cannot live. Thus the most direct way of removing fat from the abdomen is to establish a
healthy system of muscle there. As the muscles grow the fat diminishes. A man may box
and fence, and even walk, without losing his
terrible abdominal accumulation; but if he
centres his efforts at muscular exertion on the
abdomen itself the fat cannot stand the attack
and will gradually disappear.

To regain muscular control of the abdomen
after the control has once been lost is no easy
matter. The ability to contract the abdomen
observed in persons properly conditioned seems
wholly impossible to a person with much fat.
It is only by slow degrees that this control
can be regained.

The reflex action of health in the abdominal
muscles, and the proper exercise of these muscles in connection with those of the spinal and
pelvic regions, will be immediate and considerable. All the digestive tonics that were ever

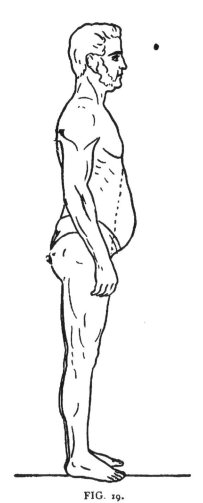

FIG. 19.

Showing fatty abdomen and extent
of reduction necessary under training.

invented cannot compete with muscular activity in the digestive region as a means of driving away ills in this region. As a direct means of accomplishing this end the treatment of the abdomen itself is obviously better than exercising in a general way, and infinitely better, of course, than the most heroic system of dieting.

One who follows conscientiously the exercises outlined in the preceding chapters, and who preserves a general activity of the muscles of the body, can never become corpulent, and for those who have just begun to acquire more than a proper or comfortable proportion of fatty material in the body, these general exercises will be sufficient to check and repair the damage. But in this chapter I have in mind those who are too corpulent for comfort and whose immediate concern is in reducing their weight. For these the following series of exercises has been arranged :

First—Contract the abdominal muscles and endeavor to draw the abdomen in and out, without breathing, until entire control of the muscles is secured. If at the beginning it is found impossible to use the muscles in this way press in the abdomen with the hands as far as possible, and while holding it thus, take several long breaths, resisting any temptation to allow the abdomen to move with the breathing. Pursue this plan until the abdomen can be drawn in and released by the action of the muscles and without the assistance of the hands.

Second—Take the correct standing position (as nearly as may be possible), and straightening the arms bring them forward and upward as far as they may be carried without hollowing the back. In reaching loosen all the muscles of the shoulders that will allow the fullest extension of the arms. The reach should be made forward and upward without removing the heels from the floor, and should be accompanied by a long breath. The motion should be repeated about ten times in a minute and will be found to have a very beneficial effect on the neck, shoulders and chest, while strengthening the lungs.

FIG. 20.

Showing fatty abdomen as distended in bending without control
of muscles.

FIG. 21.
Illustrating third exercise.

Third—Clasp the hands over the abdomen, drawing it in to the utmost; take a long breath and bend *at the hips* until the body (without bending the back) is at right angles with the legs as in Fig. 21. Straightening again, the breath should be released without relaxation of the abdomen. This motion should be repeated ten or fifteen times in a minute. Its influence will be valuable in establishing a control over the muscles.

• *Fourth*—Swinging exercises, as explained on pages 73 and 74.

Fifth—Swinging and bending exercise as described in Figs. 15 and 16. With a person of much flesh it will be impossible to touch the floor as in Fig. 16. But stoop in the general direction shown by the figure, and carry the movement as far as may be possible. Before stooping contract t h e abdomen, especially avoiding the tendency to distend it in reaching over.

Sixth—Lie flat on the back, with the hands across the abdomen, take a long breath, and raise the legs (with knee joints stiffened) until they reach right angles with the body. This must be practiced without arching the back or allowing the pelvis to leave the floor.

Seventh—Lie in the same position with the feet under the edge of a sofa, or some other object that may hold the feet against the floor, and, without the assistance of hands or elbows, raise the body into a sitting posture, at the same time contracting the abdomen.

Eighth—In the standing position : Raise one knee after the other in exaggeration of the action of going up stairs, keeping the body meanwhile perfectly erect, and practice until the knees can strike the chest. The exercise will be very beneficial in reducing flesh on legs and abdominal region.

Ninth—Dropping on the heels as described on page 79.

Tenth—Bending and touching floor as described on pages 63 and 65. A person of much flesh can only attempt this movement, but repeated practice will steadily increase the ability to bend. Have in mind here, as in all other

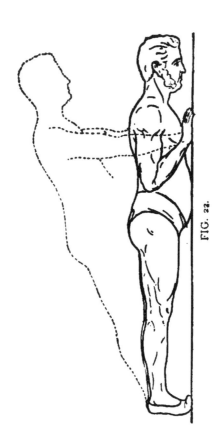

FIG. 22.

exercises, to keep muscular control of the ab-domen. Such habits will gradually diminish, its size.

Eleventh—Neck motions as described on pages 77 and 78.

Twelfth—Lie face downward on the floor —or, in consideration of that protrusive paunch— get on the hands and knees, then extend ·the body on hands and toes as in Fig. 22. Keep the body perfectly rigid—not permitting the abdomen to sag and not bending the hips up-ward to lighten the strain on the muscles. To take this position for a few seconds is all that very heavy persons will be able to do at the beginning. The exercise itself consists in low-ering the suspended body by the bending of the arms until the face touches the floor, and the effort should be repeated until this move-ment can be accomplished several successive times.

All that has been said in previous chapters about the carriage of the body will apply with equal if not greater force in the case of corpulent people. Persistently subdue the abdomen and give the prominence to the chest. Walk with the whole body, and do not move as if afraid of jarring s o m e internal machinery. Give the hips free play, and in walking—the more of this the better—practice the contraction of the waist muscles. In this way a continuous training—the only training t h a t is effectual—is kept up, and the result will be immediate and lasting.

It is to be remembered t h a t all the fat of the abdomen is not superficial like most of the other fat of the body, but is largely internal. Yet this internal fat is susceptible of reduction by pressure and exercises, and should not be encouraged to increase in bulk.

VIII.

TRAINING FOR WOMEN.

IT has already been suggested in these chapters that the exercises outlined applied as well to the training of women as to the training of men. I do not think any of the exercises described need be forbidden the gentler sex. The muscular and bone systems of men and of women are so much alike that what is good exercise for one is, except in cases of particular weaknesses, good exercise for the other. There are, however, certain of these exercises that women, especially if their health is not fair, should enter on with caution. This is all the admonition that need be made. Avoid the chances of shock to the pelvic region. Avoid also the chance of strain. If an exercise seems to make a great demand on any of the muscles, acquire perfection in that exercise by degrees.

being content to gradually acquire control of
the stiffened fibres and joints.

This suggestion would be unnecessary if so
large a proportion of woman kind did not
neglect the simplest principles of bodily health.
The "weaker" sex would occupy no such
position of relative weakness if natural laws
were followed. If women must, as is so freely
claimed, remain physically short of man's
strength, there is no reason why the disparity
should remain so great as it often is. Where
women lead an active life their strength and
endurance comes remarkably close to the
strength and endurance of the other sex, and
in the control of their own systems may readily
under development excel the other sex. In
other words, tradition has more to do with the
"weakness" of women than has nature.

It is very doubtful whether very much can
be done for the development of physical
strength and the higher health in women until
something is done toward materially reforming
women's clothing. I think I hear the reader
say, "More harping on dress reform!" But the
harping must be kept up until the shackles of

badly designed clothing are stricken from long
suffering womankind.   Then profitable training
may begin.

At the very threshold of healthful development is the obstacle of the corset.   Yes, I know
that the corset is not so tight as it used to be.
Perhaps women no longer lash their corset lace
to the bedpost and throw their weight against
it.   But even a snugly fastened corset is an injury.   Is not the proposition to remove the
corset met by the suggestion that "we could
not hold ourselves up without it?"   There lies
the mischief.   A corset that supports the back,
that keeps the back from supporting itself, is
antagonizing the first principle of physical development—the perfect muscular possession of
the body.   It is quite clear from what I have
said about carrying the body that any such
system can make no terms with the corset.
For the corset as a bust support there are now
a score of excellent substitutes.   Women might
reasonably distrust all "supports" save when
there is no evasion of this method.   In very
slender women, with slight bust measure, nothing aids development like honest chest expan-

sion and the strengthening and enlarging of breast muscles. The entire region of the chest is rendered flabby and unhealthy by any support of the central region of the body. On the other hand, fleshy women tempt increased flesh in refusing to develop the torso muscles, by incasing themselves in e nervating corsets that "hold them up" and foster increased fat.

In the case of the bust it is of importance to remember that there is here, as in all other parts of the body, a muscular system. The muscles of this region are, of course, almost invariably unlocated by their owner, and most supports soon leave them unused also. Now, by persistent effort a control over these muscles may be established until it will be possible to voluntarily contract and relax them, with the result that a sunken and flabby bust may be made full and firm. Thus, unless she is absolutely deformed, there is no reason why a woman s h o u l d not develop and mold her entire form by s i m p l y acquiring muscular control of the parts deficient in contour. The gaining of this control requires a distinct effort of will, but the results surely justify the effort.

One of the direct results of corset wearing is the curving of the spine, the tendency to hollow the chest and protrude the abdomen. The accompanying illustration prea ches a better sermon than could be put in words.

It has already been said that the corset has forced women to breathe somewhat better than men, but women are not less under the necessity of cultivating deep breathing—long breathing. They are early rendered breathless. The disappearance of the corset and cultivation of more pliant and vigorous bodies would tend to encourage more vigorous breathing. Fortunately there is every reason to believe that the corset is going out of fashion. A great many physicians, by way of rebuke, perhaps, to exaggerative remarks by those who have sought to fight the corset, are inclined to pooh-pooh the idea of its dangers. Of exaggeration there has been plenty, but the truth remains that the corset has exerted and does exert not only a direct deforming influence, but an indirect deforming influence on the whole body. It threatens the very basis of health, a ready circulation of the blood. The distended abdo-

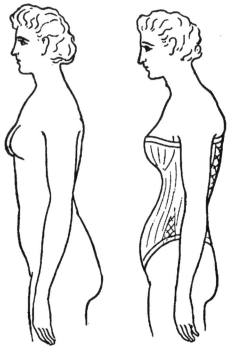

FIG. 23.

This illustration excellently exemplifies the influence of corsets on the carriage and vigor of the body. The fact that corsets are loose enough not to interfere with the breathing will not prevent the deformities naturally resulting from any contrivance for "holding up" the body. When the body holds itself up the spine becomes strong and graceful in curve. bustles are unnecessary, the abdomen is not protruded, the chest strengthens, the bust is enlarged by the development of muscles, as well as by the better arch of the breastbone, and the general grace and health of the body is immensely increased. Fleshy women will reduce their weight by increasing the activity of the muscles that should support the body.

men so shocking to women, and the great increase of flesh on the legs and feet, are often
directly due to the seizures of the corset. The
corset is naturally a constant obstacle to free
play of the body, to facility in stooping and
turning, and tends generally to curb the exercise of the sex.

Among women who have borne children,
and particularly a m o n g women who have
reached or passed middle age, the distended
abdomen often brings much distress. Nothing
certainly could be uglier, more utterly destruc-
tive of grace or distinction in manner. Tight-
ened corsets, that ludicrous last resort of the
corpulent, only increases the difficulty. The
only direct and effective way of fighting this
corpulence is, as I have said in the preceding
chapters, by getting muscular control of the
abdomen. Cast aside the corset and practice
the contraction and expansion of the muscles
while holding the breath, and follow all of those
exercises that keep active the muscles of the
pelvic and abdominal region. Do not be afraid
to bend the body.

There is no beneficial exercise that women

so seldom indulge themselves in as high reaching. The average woman is not dressed so as to be able to reach over her head. The result is that very few women know the luxury of muscular freedom in this direction. Reaching may be wrenching, and women should not, in acting upon this suggestion, rashly strain themselves in any way. High reaching with both hands, upward and forward, is very beneficial for both slender and fleshy people. This exercise is actually combined with the breathing exercises given in the chapter on breathing. It should be frequently tried and will be found very strengthening.

Women are often ridiculed in their efforts to throw a ball. They have defended themselves by arguing that their collar bone is shorter than man's. The statement is true, but women are more hampered in all such efforts by their want of familiarity with their shoulder muscles than by any brevity of the clavicle. Practice thoroughly the exercises tending to develop the shoulders and to increase the extension of the arms—not for the sake of being able to throw a ball, but for the sake of the comfort and strength derived from increased versatility in the shoulder.

An allusion has already been made to the vicious tendency of badly fitting shoes. Women are unquestionably nearer an abandonment of the corset than of the tight shoe. They admit that the Venus de Milo has a large waist. But artists who are generous in the waist-line are slow to wean from the curious tradition that the smallness of a foot is a mark of beauty. Probably ninety-five per cent. of women of all classes are suffering from small or badly designed shoes. Small shoes discourage walking and standing, and those who stand and walk little can never have a graceful carriage. If shoes are big enough the height of the heel will be a less serious affair.

It is a blessing to a large number of women that flowing skirts conceal the fact that they walk very badly. "Small shoes" is written as plainly as it could be written in the gait of the average woman. The direct influence of tight shoes on the circulation is very great. When we consider the indirect influence, induced by the retarded exercise, it is hard to credit the perverse vitality of this wretched superstition.

Women should walk more. They should not take a cab or a street car to travel half a dozen or a dozen streets. Their endurance in shopping is often a surprise to men. But the endurance is an illusion. Men intensely interested for the same length of time would appear as little fatigued. The fact is that women wreck their nervous system at "bargain counters." They should be able to bear the physical strain of standing, but their general strength is so poorly developed that they are actually unfit to do the feats they call on their nervous vitality to perform.

It seems particularly necessary to ask women in walking to turn the toes out. The in-toed proclivity among women is very curious, and has increased the tendency to an inward turn of the knees. The value of an outward turn of the toes lies not merely in any theory of force, nor in the increased strengthening of the legs, but in the influence on the pelvis. An in-toed habit encourages a contraction of the forward pelvic region—an effect whose undesirabilty need not be pointed out.

Women should, in fact, cultivate all the exercises that might give suppleness to their bodies. There can be no grace without suppleness. That complete flexibility in all the muscles of the body which the exercises enumerated have been calculated to secure is absolutely necessary to the charm of carriage which distinguishes one woman above another. Unused muscles, resulting from an absurd idea of the essential restrictions of a woman's position, are worse than no muscles, because they are irritated under tension and retard the movement begun by the muscles that are fit to use.

I believe I am the holder of somewhat radical views about the physical—not to say of the mental—possibilities of women. I have seen in China, I have seen in Germany, I have seen in England types of women, reared under certain conditions, that led me to doubt very much whether the long accepted physical inferiority of woman is indeed a fact. If it is admitted that there is no essential boundary to woman's intellectual possibilities, if she is no longer held to have an uneven chance with the other sex

in matters of the mind, I think it is probably
true that she has an absolutely even chance
with man in the development of the body. I
would ask those women who have, perhaps,
rested too greatly on the tradition of necessary
" weakness," to take this suggestion into consideration.

IX.

A WORD ABOUT CHILDREN.

WHEN an adult undertakes to train himself, begins to gain control of his muscular system and to "get strong," a large part of his labor is expended in undoing the evil of his previously acquired habits. He has to unbuild before he can build.

The muscular system has here many resemblances to the brain. Indeed, the muscles have actually a memory distinct from functions of the brain. Muscular memory is a physiological fact, and a very interesting and significant fact. Thus in the same manner that first impressions affect the brain most permanently, first habits in the muscular system cling most tenaciously to them. Habits of walking and carriage formed in childhood are very difficult

to shake off. In fact, they are all but impossible to get rid of entirely save by serious mental effort.

Nothing is more important, therefore, than
that children should be taught the general
principles of right development. It is a mere
makeshift to bring forward calisthenics. Nothing could be at the same time more amus-
ing and more pathetic than to stand in a
crowded class-room and watch the so-called
exercises perfunctorily performed by the
pupils during a few minutes of each day. But
a small minority of the children give any vigor
or meaning to the few insignificant movements
of the arms. Most of the boys, and almost all
of the girls, are found making merely superficial
movements, with no sense of the meaning and
no feeling of exhilaration. If anything has
ever been said to the children about breathing,
the chances are that no tangible impression of
the matter has been portrayed. If anything has been said about the carriage of the
body, the instructions have been confined to
an injunction to "keep back the shoulders."
In a nervous effort to keep back the shoulders

children are often found with hollowed backs
and shoulder blades driven in against the spine.

What is wanted, of course, is not backward
carriage of the shoulders, although this has
some utility, but a forward carriage of the chest.
The shoulder should not be drawn back of the
hip joint line.   There is no force in shoulders
excessively drawn backward.   If they are far
enough back to give the fullest freedom to the
development of the chest, they are in a position
to acquire all necessary strength.

Most children are wont to protrude the
abdomen in standing, and when school begins
the shoulders soon come forward.   Teach a
child to assume the correct position, giving
up whatever time may be necessary to teach
the proper line of chest and shoulders.   It
will soon forget about the correct position, but,
when reminded by a touch or word, will soon
learn to assume it, if only for a few moments,
and the habit will gradually be formed.   That
the child should know how to stand correctly,
and should assume the position at intervals,
will of itself have a good influence.

Naturally, breathing is the most important

of all features of training. Most children need very little studied exercise, but they all need specific and continued instruction in breathing. Nature has not provided for a natural development of the mind, and we have no right to assume that the body of its own accord, particularly under an artificial condition of life, acquires right habits of performing all its functions. Induce the children to take long breaths. Make them take a pride in swelling the upper chest and in drawing the abdomen in and out while holding the breath. Induce them to take deep breaths while dressing in the morning and again before going to bed, if not oftener. These habits develop by their own movement if once fairly begun. Lungs fully inflated at regular intervals will seem to call for inflation during these intervals, and involuntary deep breaths will, as I have said, gradually increase in frequency to the immense improvement of the child's lung power and general health. The *sternum*, or breast bone, is, in a child, not only divided into eight pieces, but its whole material is soft, and very little training will give a fine, swelling chest to a youngster that might other-

wise grow up flat and weak in that region.
Watch the child in sitting.   It need not be kept
stiffly seated upright.   Children should know
their position and should be able to assume it
for a few moments on occasion.   But they
should be allowed the greatest possible freedom of posture and movement.   If they bend
over a table in sitting, teach them to bend from
the hips and not from the middle of the back.
In the end this proper position will give them
much less fatigue.   Do not restrict their variety
of movement under false theories of propriety.

The superstition about women's relative
weakness begins to show itself in the training
of children.   Girls are ludicrously guarded
against exercise that they need as greatly as
boys, and at every critical period of their life
thereafter they pay in suffering for the mis-
guided consideration of those who had their
training in hand.   The so-called " lady-like "
demeanor of girls is a thing to excite impa-
tience.   Girls brought up in strait-jackets of
physical propriety—physical freedom will hurt
nobody's "manners"—can never have the grace
of deportment, the variety of poise, the readiness

in emergency that will belong to girls of liberal physical training.

As I have said, children need very little studied exercise aside from the breathing, and nothing artificial is a substitute for outdoor sport. Nothing makes better lungs than running and climbing. Excessive running is as injurious as any other excess. But frequent and easy running is one of the finest of exercises. City children do relatively little running. Girls who run are liable to be accused of rudeness (!). But country children are less under the ban of either false ideas of decorum or of restricting surroundings. City children, who do not find fences to get over, do little climbing. If it were possible to give children climbing—and arm climbing as well as leg climbing—they would be tremendously benefited in the lung region and in their entire physique.

Children are particularly in need of diverse exercise. They should not be allowed to acquire hobbies, that keep them in one line of exercise to the exclusion of other useful movements. The natural tendency of the body is to distribute strength, but habits and surroundings are continually interfering with this symmetrical growth. If children are made to do moderate exercise at spading or shoveling or sweeping, the effect upon their back will be a reward for the efforts made by both trainer and trained. *Useful* exercise thus ranks above all others, because it means something and has a double influence.

It seems scarcely necessary to speak of the importance of proper clothing. Children that are so well dressed during play hours that they are constantly occupied in an effort not to bring home any marks of dirt are in a pitiable plight indeed. Children should have play suits as well as school suits and should be forced to change from one to the other at the proper hour. Neither girls nor boys should be compelled to think of clothes at all during play hours. Imagine boys of ten or twelve avoiding kneeling positions to prevent new trousers from bagging at the knees! As for the iniquity of putting corsets on growing girls, that crime has been too often condemned to require comment here.

In his new work on " Hygiene for Childhood," Dr. Francis H. Rankin says : " Housing children during the winter months, as a precaution against them taking cold, is a very great mistake. Very few colds are contracted in the open air if the feet, limbs and body are sufficiently protected, and if the children are permitted to follow out their own inclinations of running, skipping and having free motion of the arms, *and are not exposed for too long a time to the cold.* When, however, they are compelled to walk like ' little gentlemen and ladies,' even when bundled in furs, the body soon becomes chilled if the weather is very cold, and some disturbance of the system follows. Children should be accustomed to daily exercise in the open air in all weathers, unless, of course, it is very stormy or the cold is severe, and even when delicate they should not be deprived of the tonic effects of outdoor air, and of strengthening the muscles by exercise in it. The first effect of cold air on the system is a tonic, as may be seen by the bright color in the cheeks and a feeling of exhilaration after a walk on a crisp day in autumn. Prolonged exposure to cold, on the other hand, is very depressing ; delicate children, therefore, should not remain too long out of doors if the weather is severe, or if it is very windy ; for high winds, if cool, rapidly abstract the animal heat, and are also depressing. If a child is chilled or cold, it should instantly be brought into the house to be warmed and sent out again—taking the fresh air and outdoor exercise in install ments, as it were, instead of all at once. Never permit a child to remain out of doors when crying from a cold." The last admonition might at first seem almost superfluous, but is doubtless not as entirely so as at first appears. Many indiscretions are committed on the theory of "hardening" children.

Those who have the care of children should endeavor to simply guide rather than restrict their exercise. They are certain to begin jumping sooner or later, and will certainly, until they have learned by experience, jump from points higher than they should. To avoid the chance of serious injury to the system teach little children to bend the knees and lean forward when jumping, that they may not seriously jar the spine. This may rank as precautionary training. The best exercise for children is their natural gamboling. Studied sport has not half the value. Tumbling about brings all their muscles into play, produces a general glow in their bodies and wearies them evenly.

It should not be necessary at this day to emphasize the value of sleep to children. A child that is kept up an hour too late, and excited during that hour, will need a good deal of training to overcome the bad influence of the indiscretion. In fact, if children sleep properly, eat properly and breathe properly the rest of their training is scarcely worth talking of.

X.

SOME HINTS AND SUGGESTIONS.

F, as we are so often assured, one man's food
is another man's poison, it is undoubtedly
true that a prescription of exercise for one man
or woman may be less or more than another
man or woman may require. It is utterly impossible to set down rules that might be applied
to all people alike. We may count with a good
deal of certainty upon particular characteristics
in the human form and organization, and exercise is a medicine of such universal application
that we may count definitely upon certain results from its adoption. But we cannot say
when and for how long the reader of these lines
shall follow the specific exercises. The average
person, particularly if he or she leads a busy
life, will probably find it an advantage to spend
at least fifteen minutes over particular exercises

in the morning before fully dressing, and fifteen minutes again in the evening before retiring, with another period of special exercise in the afternoon if possible, and not too close to the evening meal hour.   Of course light exercise is no detriment immediately before a meal, but if the exhilaration of practice should tempt rather vigorous movements prolonged for some time, the fatigue might not improve the appetite and would scarcely be beneficial in other respects. The entire series of movements outlined in the preceding chapters, if each is repeated ten, fifteen or twenty times, does not occupy very much time, and will leave the whole body in a pleasant glow, with no located fatigue.   The constitutional difference between one person and another will render exercises much easier to one than another.   Consequently it would be unwise to direct that any exercise should be practiced any more frequently than is rendered feasible by the muscular condition of the parts called into play.

I hope I have made it plain that the carriage and management of the body, between the

periods of specific exercise, is of more importance than the exercises themselves, and above
all that proper breathing is the very corner-
stone of physical strength. Our *habits* do more
to form our bodies as well as our minds than
the conscious efforts at improvement. So that
if we can get in the habit of taking long breaths,
and then gradually increase the length of our
respiratory movement, and the volume of air
thus taken in at a breath, we shall obviously do
more than if we arranged to merely exercise
the lungs at stated times. Stated exercises,
however, have this value, that they give special
movement to muscles and organs not commonly brought into play. Exercises, in other
words, would be unnecessary to a person who
lived a life of such physical activity that all the
muscles and organs were certain to be called
upon in the course of a day. Very few people
actually fulfill this condition. There are professional acrobats who come very close to doing it. The postman is a pretty well exercised
man, though his arms are lightly trained.
Many mechanics have excellent exercises for
the arms, legs and backs, but nothing to

strengthen the lungs and chest. The result is that they often yield to consumption in
middle life while bearing many signs of muscular strength. •It is for every person who wishes
to train himself to determine his own deficiencies as growing out of constitutional defects
or previous and present habits of life. Having
ascertained these deficiencies, it is his duty to
set about building up what remains' unbuilt or
tearing down defective elements. General
health is often threatened by one imperfection
in the system. It is customary to say that
everybody has his weak spot. The difficulty is
that most people have more than one. But it
does not follow that these weak spots might
not be banished by special effort.

"Why," I have heard it asked, "do doctors
give so much medicine for complaints that
might be remedied by natural means? Why
do they not tell the patient how to cure him
self, or, better still, to keep himself well?" The
reason is, I believe, that most physicians weary
of perpetual admonition. Their suggestions
are not received until danger appears in actual

illness.   A person who is fairly well smiles at
the doctor's criticism.   When he is on his back
the doctor's word is law.   The mystery of a
prescription has some charm in it.   Above all,
doctors do not give patients directions for
working out their own salvation without medicine, because they know that in an immense
and hopeless majority of cases the patient will
never take the trouble.   They follow directions
for a week and abandon their good resolutions.
The doctor's practical an˙ directly applicable
remedy does not appeal to the imagination.
There is no Latin in it.

The newspapers have recently contained
some talk the purport of which was that Mr.
Chauncey M. Depew, Senator Evarts and other
prominent men kept marvelously good health
without taking any more exercise than they
could help.   Mr. Depew and Senator Evarts
may have kept very good health, but they have
not done so *because* they have taken no exercise.   They have kept well *in spite* of the fact,
and observers should keep this in mind.   But,
notwithstanding the assertion, both Mr. Depew

and Mr. Evarts âre very active men. Their activity may not take the form of hard riding or walking, but they are nevertheless active. The physiologists tell us that the reason a cat keeps slender in spite of her general outward inactivity is, that her muscular system is, in fact, constantly active. If she does not make many violent movements, she is almost constantly on the alert. The nervous activity of some people wastes without building up. With others the quiet activity produces much the same effect as outward activity. The actual explanation of good health with little apparent activity is probably a union of highly perfect organs and a fortunate habit of carrying and using the body. This habit, natural to some— and a very few—must be acquired by the majority like any other element of education. Peculiar natural gifts should not mislead the majority into carelessness.

From the theory advanced it will be clear that the general hints which I have scattered through these chapters are quite as important to the perfection of training under this system

as the specific instructions which I have given
in connection with the exercise.   In all candor
it must be said that there is no substitute for
taking pains.   Bad habits are generally stronger
than good habits, and control of the muscular
system of the body will in many cases mean a
lively struggle with long established habits.
The will, which possesses so marvelous a control over the muscles, must be brought to bear
upon injurious habits of walking, of standing,
of sitting and of breathing.   It must render those
who would be strong and well persistent in
their treatment of the difficulty.   It must force
the body, in the face of hurry-scurry or of
lassitude, to yield itself to necessary special
exercises.

Head-tired people and muscle-tired people
are in two different classes.   What is recreation
for one is not recreation for the other.   It is
notorious that head-tired people are likely to
shrink from the very exercise that they should
seek.   Head-weariness produces a tendency to
avoid all initiatory movements.   At the same
time the shrinking of the head-tired person is, to

a certain extent, prompted by a necessary caution. The exercise taken up by a person who
has been exercising the brain without the body
should be exercise that animates the body
without taxing the brain. It should be exercise of a kind requiring little fatiguing thought,
though the changed attention has its value in
relieving the brain. Exercise taken by a person
who has been undergoing no serious tax on the
brain system might profitably keep up a lively
union between the intelligence and the muscles. Stimulus will help a *worried* mind, but
when the mind has performed a great deal of
detailed labor excitement of any kind is not a
good thing. 'Sleep is much better.

It is to be hoped that no new system of
training will ever send walking out of fashion.
Walking is in every respect a beautiful exercise,
especially when the walker walks as he should,
breathing slowly through the nose. Running,
as I have said, is an exercise of the highest
value to the lungs. When I run for a few
streets on a city thoroughfare, the populace
look after me as if I were a " freak," or as if I

were making off with something not belonging to me. To excite notice and even suspicion is not encouraging to the average enthusiast. People living in a city are constantly under surveillance. They are not completely at liberty. Mind and body are under the restrictions imposed by the crowd. But men, yes, and women, *should* run. Occasionally they do run in great excitement, and in no proper way, to catch a street car or a ferry boat, and reach their seat breathless, heated and uncomfortable. This is not profitable running. If people kept themselves in trim for light running it would be no such disaster to hurry for the car.

People who complain at a little climbing should be reminded that the exercise, in any kind of moderation, is highly beneficial. Nothing could be better for the lungs. A recollection of this fact will actually make labor lighter for those who keep it in mind. The flight of steps leading to an elevated railroad station should afford only reasonable exercise to a person. Stair-climbing is, indeed, a livelier exercise than at first appears, and the fatigue it brings upon people with weak legs and feeble lungs is not surprising. The weight carried in mounting an ordinary flight of steps is equal to a very considerable exertion of lifting. People who are not strong should thus not climb stairs too rashly, while they might make it an admirable means of building up their strength. In all such movements take the exercise without sudden or taxing motions. Step firmly and carry the chest free so that long, full breathing may buoy the body in its journey. Attention to the suggestions of this book will take a good many of the terrors out of stair climbing.

The shoulders should not be held back so far as to be brought out of line with the hip joints. To carry them as far back as possible, and at high tension, does not improve the force or beauty of the figure, though certain actors and military men seek to make themselves imposing in this way. The chest must be given prominence on its own account, and the shoulders, when held far enough back to give the chest free development, find a natural and comfortable centre.

Any tailor will confess that few if any of his customers have shoulders that are held precisely alike. The dressmaker tells the same story. Almost everybody has a low shoulder. This is the result of habits more or less complicated. Many people acquire a habit of contracting certain muscles when walking. One shoulder is held slightly higher than the other, the head is carried a little to one side, and one foot has slightly the advantage of the other in the labor of walking. Sometimes this trait is carried to grotesque extremes until a positive and palpable deformity is the outgrowth. In nervous people these habits are particularly frequent, and are observed in standing and sitting, and walking. In the growth of the body, in the waste and renewal of tissue, such habits are exaggerated by a steady development. Often they are the result of seemingly trifling habits like leaning to one side while sitting, or carrying a valise, or a book, or anything of the kind always in one hand. To counteract these tendencies cultivate the habit of alternating the use of the hands and arms. Watch for tendencies toward right or left-sided movements in sitting. Endeavor to adopt a changed position, which will give a relief to the wearied muscles of the desk-worker. To correct a want of uniformity in the shoulders adopt this plan : Several times a day lift the low shoulder as high as possible, holding it there, for a few moments. A regular practice of this movement will slowly increase the height of the shoulder, and in a few weeks the shoulders will be found to come into harmony. A shoulder may be too high as well as too low, though this is less often the case, and the exercise in such a condition should be to draw down the high shoulder while the other is elevated, giving particular attention to the shoulder that most needs correction. The trouble with the high shoulder is probably a continued contraction of the muscles under a nervous habit. Relaxation is then all that need be sought. Endeavor (as I have previously urged,) to develop firm and self-reliant shoulders. There are many muscles in the upper back, shoulders and chest of which you have never discovered your ownership.

The simple *stretching* of the body is a great boon. How delightful to extend all the limbs and arch the back after long confinement! Stretching movements are very serviceable in preserving suppleness. A variation upon exercises already suggested might be a purely upward reach at a wall, first with one hand and then the other, and then with both, avoiding, of course, harsh straining in the first efforts.

Of course the best kind of exercise is the exercise the body receives in performing some useful service. If a person feels that he is getting some good out a certain kind of work he has more enjoyment in that work than if he considered it either harmful labor or labor that was merely obligatory. It is notorious that men will enter with enjoyment on active sport that makes a considerable demand upon their strength, when a hod of coal hurts their back, and a little spading in the garden fills them with aches for a week. As a matter of fact, too, work done without interest actually strains the body more than work enthusiastically performed. It might, therefore, be commended

that people cultivate the habit of themselves
performing little physical tasks such as might
ordinarily be relegated to servants or hired
assistants of other kinds.   A woman who sweeps
and dusts, lifts and moves a little with reasonable caution, and makes a couple of beds of a
morning, has taken exercise in a practical and
valuable way.   A man who does not hesitate
to move a few office chairs with his own hands,
who carries a few heavy ledgers, or lends a
hand (without rashly overtaxing his strength)
in moving a piece of merchandise, has done
better than coddle himself all day, and afterward seek artistic measures of repair.   In other
words, exercise by rule need only supplement the natural exercise, which would be
better if everybody could manage to get it.
When once the body is *alive*, when all the
muscles are healthy and control of the entire
system is complete, a very little exercise, if it
be continuous, is sufficient to keep a person
healthy and strong.   I am no believer in the
theory of extensive destruction in tissues to
secure health.   This method seems to me to
threaten the wearing out of the body before it

should wear out.   It is abnormal.   As has been suggested, the lower animals keep their strength for the most part with light exercise, and some of the very strongest with extremely little animation of moment.   The tendency of hard exercise is hard muscles, and hard muscles are bad.   The body should remain firm, but pliant and in most parts soft.   It is in the conservation of energy, and not in prodigal dissipation of energy, that the greatest strength and endurance of the body will always lie.

Whenever I am asked what sort of gymnastics should be taken up by those who wish to carry exercise beyond the lighter or rudimentary forms outlined in my system of training I have always recommended tumbling, which is, after all, nearest to the natural gamboling of children and of animals, in what is vaguely called the "state of nature."   The suggestion may seem rather startling to many.   A back somersault appears like a very formidable feat to many quiet people.   But it is not so hard as it looks, and there are scores of beneficial feats of the body that may be followed with no ap-

pliances and with great benefit to the general
health.

___

The more vigorous gymnastics should be
carried on under an instructor who may render
the training symmetrical. The series of exercises outlined in this book will produce a very
general development of the system, but there are
exercises upon which the uninstructed may rashly enter without stopping to consider the chances
of uneven development. It is a well-known
principle that gymnastics produce as well as
cure deformities. The deforming influence of
fencing carried to excess must be offset by
special training calculated to give the left side
a harmonious relation to the right. Left hand
fencing, well proportioned to the amount of
fencing done with the right hand, is the best
of all cures for the mis-balanced condition
produced by ordinary practice. Boxing, if it is
not turned into "slugging," is a fine exercise.
It gives balance and suppleness to the whole
body. Yet even boxing, if the same hand is
always used for guarding, and the left shoulder
is always lifted in the protection of the head, will

produce one-sidedness to a certain degree unless off-set by other exercise. To a certain extent boxing is an off-set to fencing, the left arm being here kept high, where the right arm is high in fencing. To a certain extent the left shoulder development in boxing is an off-set to the prominence of the right shoulder in many other exercises necessary and artificial. In rowing the shoulders receive even development. Few exercises are carried to greater excess than rowing. The work is very heavy, and is frequently carried to dangerous length. Rowing properly done, and accompanied by proper training in other respects, has a great capacity for shoulder and chest development, but it is an exercise that demands great discretion, and is at best liable, in itself, to give an uneven development. Wrestling, probably the most violent of all exercises, is injudicious for most people, unless they are in good condition, and in a competition that is fairly even.

A writer makes an interesting reference to trials of endurance. He says: " Exercise of endurance is characterized by the necessity for

perfect equilibrium between the intensity of
muscular effort and the power of resistance of
the system. Now there is nothing so variable
as the power of resistance of each individual.
So that which is for one man an exercise of
strength, or of speed, becomes for another,
stronger or better trained, a simple exercise of
endurance. A canter is an exercise of speed
for a cart horse, used only to walk ; it is an
exercise of endurance for a thoroughbred, which
can sustain this pace all day without stopping.
Rowing seems an exercise of strength to a man
who is learning ; after a quarter of an hour he
is out of breath. For a waterman it is an exercise which he can, perhaps, keep up a whole
day without any fatigue."

———

"Staying power" is directly related, yes,
directly regulated by the strength of the lungs.
There can be no endurance in a weak-lunged
person, and strong lungs are thus the first and
pre-eminent requisite in one who wishes to
keep strong and be ready to enter to under-
takings of any kind that tax the physical
system. I may seem to reiterate a good deal

this necessity for lung development as a prime
factor, but the necessity seems to exist, for few
modern systems of training are giving anything
like the necessary attention to direct lung
training. They talk about big chests but little
about big lungs. Men with fine looking chests
often have treacherous lungs, a condition resulting from a cultivation of superficial strength.
*The chest must be enlarged by the expansion
of the lungs*, and not by muscular distension.
A chest made full by muscular action is a chest
traveling on false pretenses. It seems to mean
fine lungs underneath but two often does not.

There is a point to be noted in connection
with the kind of exercise suitable for persons
of different constitution and different age.
Young people of ordinary health, and no trouble with the heart, will enjoy and will profit
by quick exercise—exercises of speed. But old
people, or people suffering from debility or
breathlessness, should cultivate that which
slowly arouses their system and does not tax
their systems. Running is good for all who can
possibly accomplish it, but a long walk is much

better for a person debilitated by age, illness
or excesses, and all exercises taken by such
persons should be slow and firm rather than
lively. Exercise for such persons should, in
fact, be *persistent* rather than vigorous.

———

One year of good exercise will do more for a
woman's beauty than all the lotions and pom-
ades that were ever invented. Interesting as
are the changes produced in a man by proper
physical training, the change in a woman is
more striking and significant. Exercise seems
to have a particularly immediate effect on a
woman's complexion. I have witnessed simply
marvelous changes in the complexion, form
and disposition of women under light training.
I have in mind one well-built girl who carried
herself poorly, breathed badly and had an un-
satisfactory complexion. She joined a gymnasium, taking the lighter exercises, and began
walking a good deal. In a few months a remarkable change had been produced. The
unanimated pose had disappeared, the breathing was better (though still not what it should
be, no special training having been directed to

to the lungs), and the complexion was so clear
that one could scarcely credit the change.
Under my own training I have watched most
interesting changes as a result of breathing
exercises alone, and the extent to which locally
directed exercises have improved forms that
were considered hopeless would not be believed
save by observation.

People suffer a great deal from creduility in
following this and that random prescription
about air and exercise without stopping to
study out the natural bearings of the case.   In
just the same manner as they take up violent
and unnatural exercises in order to accomplish
what much milder forms might give them, they
take sudden and radical means of improving
their diet and getting fresh air.   Probably the
feeling with regard to hard exercise is that it
will get them strong in a hurry—a chance that
precisely suits the American plan of existence.
The suddenly rich American in the west, who
bought a whole hotel just to get a sleeping
place for one night, was the kind of man who
might plank down a roll of bills and say to

some trainer, "See here, I want to be made a full-fledged athlete by to-morrow noon!" The thing can't be done, of course. In the same way people, who have been sleeping all their lives with their bedroom window tightly closed, hear of some remarkably healthy person who invariably opens the whole upper part of his window at night. They hear it explained that we must have absolutely pure air at night. So and so almost sticks his head out of the window when he sleeps and wakes up with icicles in his beard. Presto! the hearers pull down their windows half way, determined to get this remarkable exhilaration at once. They have not been breathing ice cold outer air all day, but it must be a good thing, for so and so is in such remarkable vigor! The result, of course, is a very bad cold in the head if not something worse. Nature refuses to tolerate such surprises. Again, the rough and tumble of a Russian bath to a person not in condition for the ordeal, may mean a whole season of neuralgia. A person with delicate ears should never take the cold plunge after steam without using cotton to prevent shock to

the delicate system of those organs. As for
dieting, that is too long a story to take up
here. It seems very easy to persuade people
that every thing they eat is poison to their
particular stomach, and the credulous suffer
many a hungry pang in following out a scheme
suggested by the last friend they spoke to on
the subject. Everything but exercise is tried
in the effort to cure a sluggish stomach. There
are periodical efforts on the part of the human
family to "get back to nature," as they call it.
Getting back to nature seems to mean going
to extremes. The hermit tries going barefoot
and living on apples and barley. Animals
have no artificial covering, and men frequently
make spasmodic efforts to get rid of clothes.
They get the influenza, but hold fast to the
theory. The vegetarians, and water-curists,
and all the other theorists—many of them with
excellently founded ideas—too often get back
to nature by quarreling with their own state.
Few people try getting back to *our* nature instead of some abstract kind of animal nature.
We are what we are, and every system of training must begin with us as we are before it can

make us anything better. My own plan attempts, at least, to build up the human system on the basis of what it already is, and, by making the best of what the system already is, instead of ignoring its limitations, to build up something more enduring.

————

A cheerful fact is, that nobody need consider himself unfit for training. I was born a weakling. Nobody thought I was really worth rearing. To-day I can lift three men, each weighing one hundred and fifty pounds, and trot with them for a hundred yards. If I had not been born a weakling my family would never have taken the trouble to make me, and I would never have taken the trouble to make myself, physically what I am. If Demosthenes had not been a stammerer he might never have made himself the greatest orator of Greece. If you are weak to-day let your resentment of the fact give you the mental strength to make yourself physically sound and strong. If you are what you are, it is scarcely an exaggeration to say that you can become what you wish to be.

The repugnance to exercise arising from mental fatigue, or long inaction, is something that must be carefully fought. What is often mistaken for physical fatigue is nothing of the kind, but rather an opposite effect, the numb pain of inactivity. It will frequently be found difficult in a person of confining pursuits to arise from this state and enter upon even simple bodily exercise. But the inclination to sink into lassitude must be stubbornly fought against. The weariness is of the head and only of the body by reflex action. Once aroused from this condition a person who starts his blood at a quicker pace feels greatly stimulated. The body becomes alive again, and all the functions of the body and mind give a sense of enjoyment. No magic ever worked more agreeable results than the quickened action of the blood. The body becomes warmer, and with increased warmth comes increased strength, courage and perception. The machinery of the brain turns out more ideas to the minute under a quick pulse than under a slow one. This relationship of a quickened circulation to the powers of the brain is, perhaps, frequently over-

looked. Writers can always take advantage
of blood influence by introducing exercise
when the brain force grows weak. In prolonged mental effort recesses filled with good
general exercise, that starts the entire blood
system, will always be a better method of
alleviating the tension and tiding over the dangerous places than the use of any kind of liquid
stimulant. When stimulants aid they aid by
giving heat and artificial activity to the circulation. Exercise will supply heat in the safest
manner and leave no drafts to make good on
the bank account of strength. Stimulants are
borrowed heat. Exercise is earned heat.

———

Some pertinent remarks on ventilation and
clothing by that sagacious and wholesome
writer, Dr. Felix L. Oswald, may be quoted
here : "As houses have been called exterior
garments, a heavy suit of clothes might be
called a portable house—a protective barrier
between the skin and the cold air ; but in warm
weather the most effectual device for diminish-
ing the benefit of out-door exercise. Between
May and October man has to wear clothes

enough to keep the flies and gnats from troub-
ling him : a pair of linen trousers, a shirt and a
light neckerchief—whatsoever is more than
these is of evil.   The best head-dress for summer
is our natural hair ; the next best is a light
straw hat, with a perforated crown.   Hats and
caps, as protection from the vicissitudes of the
atmosphere, are a comparatively recent inven-
tion.   The Syrians, Greeks, Romans, Normans
and Visigoths wore helmets in war, but went
uncovered in time of peace in the coldest and
most stormy seasons ; the Gauls and Egyptians
always went bare-headed, even in battle, and
a hundred years after the conquest of Egypt by
Cambyses (B. C. 525), the sands of Pelusium
still covered the well-preserved skulls of the
native warriors, while those of the turbaned
Persians had crumbled to the jaw-bones.   The
Emperor Hadrian traveled bareheaded from the
icy Alps to the borders of Mesopotamia ; the
founders of several monastic orders interdicted
all coverings for the head ; during the reign of
Henry VIII. boys and young men generally
went with the head bare, and to the preservation of this old Saxon custom Sir John Sinclair

ascribes the remarkable health of the orphans
of the Queen's Hospital. The human skull is
naturally better protected than that of any
other warm-blooded animal, so that there
seems little need of adding an artificial covering ; and, as Dr. Adair observes, the most
neglected children, street Arabs and young
gypsies, are least liable to disease, chiefly because they are not guarded from the access of
fresh air by too many garments. It is also
well known that baldness is the effect of effem-
inate habits as often as of dissipation ; and yet
there are plenty who think it highly dangerous
to let a boy go out bareheaded even in May or
September. The trouble is, that so many of
our latter-day health codes are framed by men
who mistake the exigencies of their own de-
crepitude for the normal condition of mankind.
Thousands of North American mothers get
their hygiene oracles from the household notes
of some orthodox weekly, where the Rev. Fal-
staff Tartuffe assures them—from personal experience—that raw apples are indigestible, and
that rheumatism can be prevented only by
night-caps and woolen undershirts."

The same wholesome writer expresses a
sentiment with which I fully agree and cannot
forbear to quote : " What a stimulous it would
give to manly sports and manly virtues, nay,
to the physical regeneration of the human
race," says Dr. Oswald, speaking of the Turn-
bund and organized sports, " if we could make
their yearly assembly a national festival !   The
river-meadows of Chattanooga, on the moun-
tain amphitheatre near Huntsville, Alabama,
would make a first-class Olympia, and our
Indian s u m m e r would be a ready made
'weather-truce,' without an expensive burnt
offering to the sun.   Olives, it is true, do not
flourish on our soil ; our mercenary souls need
other inducements ; but the rent of reserved
seats and camp tents would enable us to gild
the crowns of the several victors.   Imagine the
athletes of every village training for the prizes
—thousands of boy-topers turning gymnasts,
ward delegates running for something besides
office, and the Young Men's Christian Association seeking paradise on this side of the
grave !"

Physical health must, indeed, become something more than a mere fad before our race can do itself justice in the eternal struggle for higher ideals. It is only pedantic cowardice that says we are physically going backward ; but it is true wisdom to acknowledge the danger of allowing modern ignorance of the human body to long continue its dangerous effects.

APPENDIX.

A WORD ABOUT THE SPINE.

BEFORE saying anything of the spine as a feature of the human system to be trained or modified, let us see what the spine is from the anatomist's point of view.

If we go to a work like the "Anatomy" of Gray we shall find a satisfactory account of the spine from the historical and surgical sides; that is to say, an account of the spine as it has been and is in the average specimens of the human family taken for dissection, or examined with a view to gaining accurate knowledge of actual conditions. It is not the business of the anatomist to be a prophet. He is not concerned with the spine as it might be or should be. He is called to consider it as it is. I will not apologize here for giving briefly some information about so important a feature of the body as the spine. In fact, such

a course is absolutely essential if the suggestions to be offered concerning the training of
the spine are to be understood.

The spine is described as a flexuous and
flexible column, formed of a series of bones
called vertebræ (*vertere*, to turn.) Its average
length is about two feet two or three inches.
There are thirty-three of the vertebræ. They
are divided by name into cervical, dorsal,
lumbar, sacral and coccygeal vertebræ. As
will be seen by the accompanying illustration,
seven of these bones are found in the cervical
or neck region ; twelve in the dorsal or upper
back region ; five in the lumbar or lower back
region ; five in the sacral or pelvic region, and
four comprising the. rudimentary tail of which
evolution has not yet deprived mankind.

Speaking generally of the vertebræ Gray
says : "The bodies of the vertebræ are piled
one upon the other, forming a strong pillar for
the support of the cranium · and trunk, the
arches forming a hollow cylinder behind for
the protection of the spinal cord. The different vertebræ are connected together by
means of the articular processes and the inter-

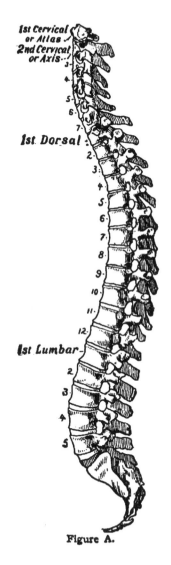

1st Cervical
or Atlas
2nd Cervical
or Axis
3
4
5
6
7

1st Dorsal
2
3
4
5
6
7
8
9
10
11
12

1st Lumbar
2
3
4
5

Figure A.

vertebral cartilage, while the transverse and spinous processes serve as levers for the attachment of muscles which move the different parts of the spine. Lastly, between each pair

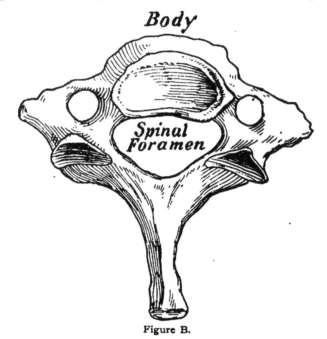

Figure B.

of vertebræ apertures exist through which the spinal nerves pass from the cord."

A fragment of vertebræ is really a complicated affair, as we may see in figure *B*, which presents a section (the seventh) of the cervical vertebræ. In figure *C* we have a group of the

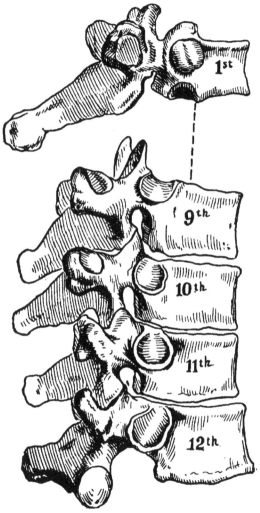

Figure C.

dorsal vertebræ. The illustration will suggest
the peculiar manner in which the bones are
fitted together. The parts in *C* bearing the
numbers represent that part of the vertebræ
which is called the *body*, and corresponds to
the parts marked *body* in *B*. A cushion of
cartilage is placed between each of these body
bones. The opening in figure *B*, marked
"Spinal Foramen," shows the avenue through
which the carefully protected spinal cord
passes. The protruding point of bone opposite the *body* is the point felt through the skin
of the back and the point to which the muscle makes its attachment.

The curve in the spine, shown in Fig. *A*, is
the one usually represented by anatomists, and
is, perhaps, the curve actually existing in the
average body. One of the general peculiari-
ties of the spine is a slight lateral curvature
toward the right, usually explained by the
preferred use of the right hand and arm. The
explanation is supported by the statement that
in left-handed persons the lateral curvature is
likely to be directed to the other side.

The curve shown in Fig. A is so general, I

might say universal, that it has come to be looked upon as inevitable. Finding this curvature so general anatomists have been ready to assume that the curve was favored by some desirability. The most familiar argument is that the curving of the spine helps to absorb vibration and saves the brain from shock. It is also urged that the curve lends greater force and strength to the spine than if it were straight.

Very young children do not have a curved spine. Their backs are perfectly flat. As they grow older and begin walking the spine begins to take on a more or less pronounced curve. If the body is carelessly carried the curve increases. In old age the curve is sometimes seen in its most pronounced form. Various causes contribute to the curvature. The muscles tend to draw the spine out of the straight line, which it readily assumes in young children. Then when the child stands the weight of its head and the upper part of the body aids the curvature, if there is no unnecessary yielding to the force of gravity. Relaxed muscles in a lazy, careless or decrepit person leave the weight of these upper parts of the body to curve the spine in an exaggerated degree.

Let us look at the claim that the curved spine is desirable and inevitable. The suggestion that the curve aids the intervertebral substance in absorbing the shock is not borne out by an examination of the structure of the spine, or by a study of natural conditions in the individual. A shock from above, sufficiently severe to call into play the elasticity of the spine, would probably break the skull. A shock from below is so largely absorbed by the muscles of the legs and pelvic region that very little of it reaches the spine itself. If this were not so walking and running would be intolerable. If the spine were actually subjected to the necessity of bearing the frequent shocks from below a person would soon become paralyzed. In any case the relation of the curvature to the whole shock-bearing capacity of the spine is too slight to justify the preservation of the curvature on the utilitarian ground.

Prof. Gray himself admits that the cushion-substance between the vertebræ is thicker at

the front than at the back in the cervical and
lumbar regions. In other words, it is thinner
on the *inside* of these sharp curves of the neck
and lower back, where the pressure is greatest,
and thickest on the *outside* of the curves
where it is slightest, as the illustration shows.
In the middle of the spine, where the bones
run in the straightest line, the cushions are
of evener form, a fact which offers a curiously
interesting argument for the general volun-
tary straightening of the spine.

The argument that
a curve gives strength
to the vertebral column
is scarcely borne out
by mechanical princi-
ples. A lateral arch
is stronger than a
straight horizontal line
with the pressure from
above. Thus, in Fig.
D, an arch with a
pressure at A is
stronger than a hori-

Figure D.

zontal support with a pressure at B. But

an upright curve, with the pressure at C, is not by any means so strong as the straight line with the pressure at D. This is a rudimentary principle of mechanics that cannot be escaped.

If neither the concussion theory nor the theory of force in support justifies the curved spine, and the curvature is explained only by the action of weight, of muscular action, and of careless carriage, then there is no reason why the curve should not be voluntarily modified, if the modification can be shown to be advantageous.

Some of the reasons why the spine should be straight, or should, at least, have as little curve as possible, have already been suggested in this treatise. It will appear that when it is straightened the general grace and force of the body is increased. The backward curve, as in Fig. 1 (p. 22), is enfeebling and forceless. The forward curve, as in Fig. 2 (p. 25), is dangerous as well as inelegant. This position naturally tips the pelvis forward. In a careless or feeble position the pelvis is sometimes too far forward—sometimes too far back.

Either position is inimical to the health of the organs and to the strength and endurance of the system as a whole. People who throw the pelvis too far forward in standing often tip it nervelessly back when sitting, with the result discussed on page 28.

The weight of the abdomen, which, in young children, begins to draw the pelvis forward, often produces the same effect in people who acquire abdominal fat. This action on the pelvis, increasing the forward curve of the lumbar region in the spine, is one of the most dangerous effects of corpulency. I would be at little difficulty in showing the shocking effects of this change in the various organs.

Thus a proper carriage of the pelvis is the first and paramount precaution against abdominal fat. The muscular action necessary to the preservation of a right angle in the pelvis discourages fatty formation in this region. As I have already said, no one who carries the pelvis in the manner described and illustrated, and who sufficiently controls the abdominal muscles, can acquire abdominal fat.

The proper angle in the pelvis is at once

a result of a straight spine and an assistance to a straight spine. Control of the abdominal muscles carries on the work the pelvis begins, and the neck muscles aid the spine itself in straightening the .shoulder and neck region; while drawing back the head, with the face vertical and parallel with upright lines of the body, increases the force of the body's position and benefits the expansion of the lungs.

MORE ABOUT BREATHING.

SINCE the original publication of this book I have received from various persons who are interested as teachers in the science of physical culture, various suggestions and criticisms upon the method of breathing advocated in the foregoing pages. One lady who taught others how to breathe according to the method in which I had instructed her, was advised not to do so by another person who claimed to be high in authority as regards what form of physical education should or should not be taught in certain quarters, urging that the system I advocated was not orthodox, and giving as a further reason why my idea should not be advocated, that I was not a professional—whatever that may mean.

The whole difficulty in the question of proper methods of breathing seems to me to rest on the failure to understand the essential

difference between costal and abdominal breathing. A great deal that is conflicting and mis-
leading has been written on this subject, both
by those who are supposed to thoroughly understand the makeup of the human animal as
well as by those who do not claim this ex-
haustive knowledge. It is not in my province,
neither have I any desire, to criticise individu-
als. I have neither the time nor the inclination
for personal debates, but so long as my own
vitality survives I shall not hesitate to attack
systems of training, be they general or specific,
that have not a basis in actual facts and natural
reason.

The subject of costal breathing, to which I
have referred in the chapter on "How to
Breathe," seems to offer one of the most press-
ing questions of the hour ; and its discussion
would be particularly valuable, perhaps, to
those who fancy themselves securely orthodox.

But before saying more of this, I must speak
of an allusion often made by people who seem
to pay more attention to developing their mem-
ories than to developing their power of reason;
I mean their allusion to the being called a

normal man and woman, by which is generally meant the primitive man and woman.

Now, this being who is held up for our guidance in physical matters as a sort of beacon which, if followed, will surely lead us poor civilized mortals into a state of serene health; who would make the *materia medica* obsolete and send into oblivion those who practice it ; this being offers, I am afraid, no very promising guide to reasonable beings. Speaking of this primitive being whom we are told to look upon as a perfect physical type, Fritz Schultz in his work on "Fetichism" aptly remarks that he has no intelligence. Such beings exert themselves only so far as strict necessity requires. After the hunt comes unbroken repose. Feast and gluttony are regarded by all primitive savages as the acme of earthly felicity. Infanticide, fœticide, abortion, abandonment, sale and even eating of children are so common among them as to explode all the sentimental idyllic tirades that have ever been sung about the innocent life of the human animal in the state of nature. All of which goes to prove that education, especially that

part of education in which the reasoning
faculties are devoloped by observation, compa-
rison and deduction is much the best factor in
developing men and women to the highest
possible point of physical as well as mental
perfection.

I do not beleive, then, in imitating the
savage. From what I have observed of these
so-called normal beings they are nothing
more than what may be best described as raw
material ; and in that state they certainly are
not models fit for us to follow, unless we wish
to retrograde. In the undeveloped state of
their intellectual powers, they know nothing of
forces of nature, and unless they **do they** cannot
hope to develope themselves physically. In
their condition they know no more of breathing so as to foster a healthy and long life,
than they do of ethical philosophy. They
breathe abdominally because they are lazy and
ignorant, and do not know how and never have
known how to breathe any other way.

This very condition is the trouble with a
majority of the people whom we call civilized.
As I have already suggested, nature no more

teaches the human animal how to breathe,
walk, stand, stoop and sit in a manner more
beneficial than may be suggested by the
promptings of our sensations, than she teaches
to read and write. One is as much a matter of
education as the other. Many writers are fond
of pointing to the case of the Indian woman
who gives birth to children without the aid of a
physician or the care of a nurse, and of claim-
ing this as proof of the Indian woman's physical superiority in a primitive condition. But in
truth the fact offers no real proof of any such
superiority, for the same conditions are frequently to be found in centres of civilized life among
people whose circumstances force or induce
them to do without the comforts of civilized
people in general. Those who care to investi-
gate, and who are willing to accept a truth
even when it destroys a pet theory, will find
that civilization causes no physical deteriora-
tion, either physical or mental, so long as people do not willfully reject knowledge.

Breathing costally, or without the action of
the abdomen, is an educated method of breathing, and can be acquired only by an earnest

and conscientious effort and a definite co-operation of the mind and body.

In acquiring this method of breathing, the first thing to be done is to learn how to hold the body erect, after the manner already explained in Chapter II. Standing seems to be the simplest possible thing to do, but the slightest observation will teach the reader that all people do not stand the same way; that some round the shoulders, that some pull them awkwardly far back, that some protrude the abdomen, and so on. All of these postures are incorrect. There is only one right way, that is, the way that enhances the strength, the endurance, the general health of the body. In Chapter II. I have sought to make plain what the correct standing position seems to me to be.

Now, practice dilating the nostrils as a horse does. Inhale slowly as much air as you can—through the nostrils, of course—and release the air again through the nostrils. At the same time slowly contract the muscles of the abdomen, contracting and releasing these muscles until the control is so perfect that the motion may be continued while the slow breathing is going on.   Meanwhile, the arms, unless they are occupied, should hang at the sides. Their muscles need not be used—they will not drop off.

To breathe costally by a conscious effort of the nostrils and the muscles of the upper chest may require and does require a conscious restraint of a tendency to use the abdominal muscles.   For the successful acquirement of this beneficial method of breathing the abdominal movement must be specifically resisted. The result is not only the strengthening of the lungs and chest, but the strengthening of the waist region.

I have elsewhere (in the chapter on training for women) alluded to the relationship between corsets and breathing.   In that chapter I have said that the fact that corsets force women in a measure to breathe costally and prevent the abdominal action was in a measure a beneficial action.   The suggestion seems to have been taken up by certain ladies eager to defend the use of the corset.   At one meeting, indeed, a lady is reported as saying, "Checkley advocates corsets."

It should not be necessary to say that I never advocated or defended corsets. The fact that corsets may in one direction be said to have had a beneficial action by no means justifies their use. As measured against the injury they do, the benefit is very meagre indeed.

The chief injury wrought by the corset results from its use as a support to the body. Anything that helps hold up the body, that prevents the body from holding itself up, is—unless in the case of cripples or hopelessly enfeebled persons—an injury to the body. The corset increases any tendency to weakness in the back. It increases and does not diminish a tendency to fleshiness. Women who, in getting into a corset, push as much flesh as possible above and below the waist line in order to decrease their circumference at the waist, are not only deforming themselves and increasing the fatty enlargement by incasing and holding it free of muscular action, but are working other positive injuries to their system.

SOME MEDICAL AND PERSONAL COMMENTS ON THE CHECKLEY SYSTEM AND "A NATURAL METHOD OF PHYSICAL TRAINING."

Original Theories.

Dr. Jos. Rodes Buchanan in the Anthropologist.

His methods and discoveries differ so widely from everything that has been done in that direction heretofore, and are indeed so marvelous, as to suggest that something more than the common reasoning power of man may have guided him as by intuition to doctrines so novel, of which there has never been a hint in any production of physicians, artists, hygienists or philosophers heretofore.

A Natural and Reasonable System.

Science.

The method of training advocated and taught in this little volume appeals at once to the good sense of the reader. It requires no machinery or apparatus of any kind, except, of course, the bones and muscles of the person training, and it may be taken up and pursued at any time and in any place, either with or without an instructor. The aim is not to pro. dace champion rowers or boxers or sprinters, nor even to develop good "all-round" athletes, but to do for the body what education does for the mind. The aim is to put the body into the best possible condition for doing the work it has to do, and to keep it in that condition. The author believes that there is more "straining" than "training" in some of the popular systems of physical training practiced in and out of the college gymnasium, and his method departs radically from those systems in many respects. But we find nothing in it that physicians could take exception to in the case of any person physically sound. The book is fully illustrated, many of the engravings being made from instantaneous photographs of the author in the different positions assumed in the course of training.

Safest, Wisest, Most Practical Method.
From Annals of Hygiene.

We are always heartily in sympathy with any system of physical culture that aims to accomplish results without the use of apparatus. Of course, *all* appliances are not to be condemned but we, quite firmly, hold that they are unnecessary. A little volume on "Physical Training," by Edwin Checkley, has recently fallen into our hands, and we have been so very favorably impressed with its teachings that we can and do strongly commend its perusal to all the readers of *The Annals.* It is a very happy thought of Mr. Checkley's, and pre-eminently correct, when he holds that "a man or woman should get good health and sufficient strength and perfection of form in the ordinary activities of life, if those activities, however meagre, are carried on in obedience to right laws." Mr. Checkley's instructions about "breathing" are particularly good. While we are not entirely in accord with the author's commendation of running, which we do not think a healthy or desirable form of exercise, with this one exception we can heartily recommend his book as containing about the safest, wisest, most physiological and most practical exposition of the subject of physical culture that we have yet encountered.

A Natural System.
New York Medical Times.

A young man educated as an engineer, and accustomed to study in his profession the harmony of parts, applies the principles thus obtained to the careful study of the most perfect machine in the world, the human body, and finds, he thinks, a solution of the question which the scientist and philosopher in the past had so long in vain tried to solve. The essence of Mr. Checkley's system is that the ordinary movements of everyday life, breathing, walking, stooping, etc., can be made to develop the body so perfectly in the routine course of everyday action, not only sufficient to prevent any unnatural and unhuman increase of size, but also to bring the body up to a full natural development, with all that vigor and beauty of motion characterized by the harmonious action of all the organs. In truth, there can be no proper training that does not educate the whole system of the man. Mr. Checkley's ideas are particularly applicable to women, not only in her movements, but especially in her dress, which, he claims, if properly carried out, will not only give a perfect form, but do away with a large portion of those pelvic diseases to relieve which a very large class of specialists are acquiring not only professional reputation but wealth. The system of Mr. Checkley promises, by the proper control of all the organs, much better results than can be obtained by the exclusion of different kinds of food. The system in its healthy condition, with each muscle and bone and tissue doing its roper work, takes up only the necessary ingredients from the food to accomplish its purpose, getting rid of the rest in the form of excrementitious material.

For Women and Children.
Medical Age.

Mr. Checkley's views are built upon practical, hard common sense. No one will lose anything by perusing this little volume, and may gain considerable desirable information. We especially commend the chapters devoted to physical training of women and children.

Deserves A Large Audience.
Anthropologist.

The book should be read by everybody.

Not for Athletics but for Health.
Medical Review.

This is just what it is claimed to be, a natural method of physical training. It is written by a man who knows his busi-

ness. It is written in a pleasing style, and is so written that
"one who runs may read."

Will Draw Everybody's Attention.

Prof. Persifor Frazer, D. S., in Journal of the Franklin Institute.

The writer of this small octavo of 152 pages comes before
the public like Francis Galton, without any title from the school
of Medicine, and, like Francis Galton, he displays a familiarity
with the structure and functions of the body which adds very
much to the charm and the convincing force of his book. He
has many points which favor him before the public, such as an
earnest and withal a very clear and pleasant style ; a subject
which interests everybody and will draw everybody's attention
so soon as the writer inspires confidence in his knowledge of the
subject, which Mr. Checkley very shortly does. Then the ·
means which he employs are simple and natural, and being
always at hand, leave the would-be physical reformer no
excuse for missing his exercise. The theory put forth by Mr.
Checkley is not new but it is very strongly stated. It is, in short,
that with the attention called to such points as the correct carriage of the body, the proper manner of breathing, and the
repetition, morning and evening, for twenty minutes or so, of
such motions as bring into play the muscles on which the daily
routine makes no demand, not only the general health and
power of sleep are improved, but also the physical strength is
greatly increased, the tendency to corpulence checked and its
unpleasant consequences avoided.

Even were there no examples of the practical success of this
system its simplicity and reasonableness would take one captive,
but the writer has seen a practicable proof of its beneficent
working on a short and very fleshy man, whose pursuits were
so little favorable to the maintenance of the well-proportioned
frame, and whose occupations were so exacting and numerous
that he had fallen into that bourne of rotundity and flaccid
muscles from which few can return. For years he had seriously projected correcting this evil by gymnasium exercise, but
had never "found the time," and was rapidly tending toward

the outline of a human sphere   Finally, this little book fell
into his hands, and he made a determined effort to follow its
precepts

Without subjecting himself to any unusual deprivation of
diet, he began rapidly to reduce his excessive corpulence, until
in three weeks his trunk had changed from the appearance of
a pear to that of a barrel, his waist measure had diminished
from forty-one inches to thirty-six and one-half, while his chest
measure had increased. A neck began to be visible ; short
breath became a nightmare of the past, and almost without
effort he assumes the proportions of an athlete

It may well be that all will not have the strength of will to
carry out this regimen so faithfully, and will not so soon reap
their reward ; but that it will prove beneficial to all is certain.
The advice it contains as to the physical training of women
and children is timely and admirable.

The writer is not acquainted with any treatise on the art of
preserving health and comfort, or of regaining them when lost,
by natural and inexpensive means, which is so sensible, so practical and so clear as this little book, which is heartily recommended to the public.

Well Worthy of Study.

New York Medical Times.

Mr. Checkley's investigations have certainly a scientific
basis, and are well worthy of that careful inquiry and experi-
ment which every physician can carry out himself.   Bismarck
and others keep down the flesh by a careful attention to diet,
but the same plan pursued by others is a complete failure.   A
careful study of the use of every organ and the proper carriage
of the body, so that each organ performs its proper function
and all work in harmony, it would seem, might be a much
more scientific and pleasant solution of the question than the
mere study of the nature and character of foods.

Incomparable.

Walter B. Gunnison, Ex-Pres. N. Y. State Teachers' Association.

I know of no book that compares with it.

Will Bear Good Fruit.

William Blaikie, Author of "How to Get Strong."

So easy to learn, and so quick in bearing results of a kind gratifying and helpful to the pupil, that you cannot fail to soon have an army of followers. If the habit of deep slow breathing which you urge can only become general it will add many per cent. to our vitality and staying powers as a nation ; while the correct carriage of the body, as taught by you, will be a boon especially to young women who wish to be graceful which can hardly be overestimated.

GENERAL PRESS COMMENTS.

New York Herald.

Worth its weight in gold.

The Journalist,

A little volume which could be read and its instructions followed with advantage by every editor, librarian or sedentary worker. His object is not to make athletes, but perfectly healthy, symmetrically developed men and women. His theory is based on careful study and common sense.

Journal of Education.

The book is thoroughly original. His philosophy is simple, and the practice based upon it is easily secured.

Buffalo News.

Appeals to common sense.

San Francisco Argonaut.

One of the best, if not *the* best, of books on practical physical training.

Detroit Journal.

We can recommend this book as of value to everybody who desires physical health.

Chicago Globe.

The book will pay any one to peruse as a means of health.

Omaha World-Herald.

At once educat'o.ial and interesting.

Toledo Bee.

Some truths worthy to be read and remembered.

Brooklyn Eagle.

A beautiful as well as a useful book. It is an invaluable little manual for those who wish to know for themselves and their children or pupils how to hold themselves, walk. or do any muscular thing in reason for which they may be called on.

Pittsburg Times.

A timely book. Mr. Checkley has laid all who appreciate the importance of physical education under lasting obligations to him.

Brooklyn Standard-Union.

In this admirable work Mr Checkley does in reality supply a "long felt want." It is the very thing a multitude of fat men and women have been looking for.

Buffalo Express.

A book which we heartily commend.

Richmond Dispatch.

Folks who find it difficult to pull on their own stockings ought to be profoundly grateful to Prof. Checkley.

Scranton Truth.

Cannot fail to set men and women thinking seriously.

Boston Journal.

Mr. Checkley has as the foundation of his system the true idea for training the body, and his book is a cleverly written and useful treatise.

Indianapolis News.

A most instructive and suggestive work. It appeals to everybody's interest.

Springfield Republican.

Will not fail of a hearing and disciples.

Grand Rapids Democrat.

Has created something of a sensation in the athletic world and among the schools of hygienic culture.

Boston Globe.

The principles are common sense ones.

Kansas City Globe.

It is a book that ought to be in every house.

San Francisco Post.

The book should be read by all athletes and by all whose business is confining.

New Orleans Sunday States.

There is an excellent chapter on training for women, and an equally good one on exercise for children.

Cincinnati Commercial.

This book is intelligently written and its thories tend away from high pressure systems.

Detroit Tribune.

Health-seekers will read it with pleasure.

University Voice.

It is a work that should be in the hands of every one who loves health.

The Wilmington Every Evening.

A very obvious advantage of the movements which Mr. Checkley prescribes and describes is that they may be performed in one's chamber or office, and they can be practiced in entire safety by any one whose physical system is sufficiently sound to warrant him in swinging his arms, moving his legs or bending his back, while to the more robust they will at least well serve as preparatory to the more vigorous athletics of Indian clubs, dumb-bells, horizontal and parallel bars, et id' genus omne. "The chest must be enlarged by the expansion of the lungs, and not by muscular distention," is the foundation upon which Mr Checkley builds, and if his book succeeds in making this one truth more generally felt it will have done a good work.

Cortland Standard.

The book of the century on the subject of which it treats.

Glen Cove Gazette.

A marvel of simplicity.

Nashville American.

Full of valuable suggestions.

Minneapolis Journal.

All who would quicken their sluggish blood will see the dvantage of this method at once.

Poughkeepsie Eagle.

Many original ideas.

Toledo Bee.

Mr. Checkley's book is leading and convincing and a study of it must result in great good. It will be of incalculable benefit to the young who are forming habits of body, and who, as everyday observation teaches us, need such a guide.

New York News.

The best manual on the subject we have seen. It does away with the use of cumbrous and costly apparatus, which more often results in muscle straining than muscle training, and lays down certain easily performed natural exercises, which can be followed without the aid of the usual paraphernalia of the gymnasium.

New York Press.

A simple and common sense system.

Public Opinion.

Among all the books that have appeared since open air exercises and athletics began their recent era of increasing popularity, there is not one that impresses the reader more strongly with the idea of primitive sense and practicability.

Journal of Packer College Alumnæ.

This book will be found very useful to mothers who have children to train, and to young girls who desire to possess a graceful carriage and supple body.

Congragationalist.

The book is one which deserves a wide reading, and many children would be greatly benefited if their parents would study and apply it.

New York School Journal.

It is a reaction against the health lift and other costly appliances once thought necessary. We commend this little volume as being a decidedly good one.

National Stenographer.

Mr. Checkley's plan comes like an inspiration and tells us how we may maintain our vigor without the usual inconveniences. . . We recommend the book most heartily to every stenographer.

Manufacturer and Builder.

To the multitude of those who are victims of the impediment of adipose, the author is the bearer of tidings of great joy.

Chicago Herald.

This system is the only one that offers a reasonable method of curing obesity, the bugbear of humanity, without rendering the subject as uncomfortable as a convict at hard labor.

The Critic.

Its great charm is its simplicity. It calls for no machinery, but rather clamors against all artificial processes. It involves absolutely no outlay in cash or pecuniary credit. It requires no gymnasium, but may be fully applied in the hall bed room of a boarding house. If you go visiting you need take no paraphernalia with you, yet can be sure of getting your daily stint of exercise. . . We commend the book.

Minneapolis Journal.

Just as well adapted to the necessities of women as of men.

St. Louis Republic.

Something really new on the subject of physical training.

Baltimore Sun.

Good sense and clear statement.

Book Chat.

A system that is not dependent upon any appliances whatever, and that will build up the frame of the slender and reduce the unwelcome proportions of the corpulent without the employment of machinery or harsh and weakening methods of dieting.

Worcester Spy.

Well worth careful study.

Albany Argus.

Should have wide acceptance. . . . . The Checkley system is founded on science and commen sense.

St John (N. B.) Gazette.

Teeming with useful knowledge.

Indianapolis Journal.

Deserves the attention of everybody interested in cultivating bodily strength.

St. John (N. B.) Globe.

A book that every man, woman and child in the world can read with profit.

New York World.

Read this and be strong.

Educational Review.

Admirable in its naturalness and the simplicity and effectiveness of method, which give it ready adaptability. . . . The growing popularity of physical culture has given us of late many interesting manuals, but none of greater value to the average lay reader than that by Mr. Checkley, which is already in its seventh edition. Beginning with the statement that most popular systems inculcate physical "straining" rather than physical "training," the author in a few well-written chapters outlines a system of his own, whose chief merit lies in the fact that it is exceedingly simple and does away with all expensive apparatus and infinitely complex details of diet and exercise.

Correct breathing is regarded as the most important element in securing a healthful development. The right carriage of the body, such as to secure the easy and natural play of the organic functions, is emphasized, while "muscle-molding" schemes that have the effect to "lay on" the exterior hard and fast masses of muscles to the detriment of the organic functions, are disparaged. Simple exercises without apparatus are suggested for the training of muscles and joints, and many useful hints are given as to what exercise can and cannot do for the upbuilding and conserving of health and bodily efficiency. The characteristic feature of the book is its advocacy of the most simple rules as regards exercise and diet.

The man who has purchased expensive physical apparatus in the hope of finding health and strength by conscientiously following out complex directions as to its use, but who has become disgusted with the tiresome burden imposed, will feel greatly relieved, on reading these interesting chapters, to discover that by attending to a few plain directions as to carriage of body, walking, breathing, and occasional flexion of important muscles, he can dispense with his complex paraphernalia, and still become a vigorous, healthy, robust person, capable of all ordinary endurance, without an unduly developed biceps and a case-hardened layer of unyielding muscle.

To the teacher of calesthenics who is looking for something novel in the way of muscular movements—"contortions," as Mr. Checkley calls them—to elicit the admiring gaze of lookers on, there will be little in this book to attract. To the lay reader who desires a brief and rational account of the *cui bono* of all the many schemes for muscle-training that are recommended as the necessary condition of a symmetrical bodily development, but who feels that life is too short to attempt to learn the new "science," this book will be a welcome boon.

Boston Journal.

Mr. Checkley has as the foundation of his system the true idea of training the body, and his book is a clearly written and useful treatise.

COMMENTS OF THE BRITISH PRESS.

Hygienic Review.

It would need a lengthy review to do justice to this excellent little work, and we cannot do better than advise our readers to procure a copy for themselves. . . . In the latter part of the work the author writes very rationally on the treatment of obesity, and training for women.

The Gymnast.

The point in what is here called "The Checkley System" is the entire absence of apparatus in its application. Briefly, this book may be described as a manual of selected extension exercises, suitable for use either by the weakly or by those who are anxious to keep in condition but have not the time or inclination for work in the gymnasium.

Yorkshire Post.

A little book likely to prove of great service to those who wish to reduce flesh naturally without dieting. A series of exercises are suggested suitable for men and women that are certainly worth testing.

Public Opinion.

"The Checkley System," which this volume seeks to set forth, seems a very practical, and, at the same time, a very simple method of acquiring good habits in the aforesaid effort. . . . The book is well gotten up, and the illustrations in the text are exceptionally good.

Anti-Jacobin.

The author's remarks on the training of girls and women are particularly apt and useful ; the diagrams which illustrate each mode of exercise help out the book considerably.

Bradford Observer.

Mr. E. Checkley advocates a rational system of exercise for men and women which would add greatly to heir strength, endurance and beauty.

Educational Times.

This is a very sensible book which deals with making muscle, and reducing flesh without dieting or apparatus . . The book is evidently written by one who knows what he is writing about. . . The illustrations are good and serviceable.

European Mail.

This book is worthy of being widely read. There is no doubt that Mr. Checkley's system is thoroughly sound and rational ; it is so absolutely convincing and in accordance with the dictates of common sense.

Dublin Evening Mail.

This is a small but useful book. . . . One can heartily recommend Mr. Checkley's work as an intelligent and con-scientious effort in the direction of usefulness and benefit to the human race.

Echo.

For ourselves we regard Mr. Checkley's views to be worthy of the most respectful consideration. His principles are rational and natural. . . Mr. Checkley teaches us how to walk, stand and breathe.

Hereford Times.

This is a capital little book on the making of muscle and reducing of flesh without dieting or apparatus. It is plainly and moderately written, every page containing some rational observation.

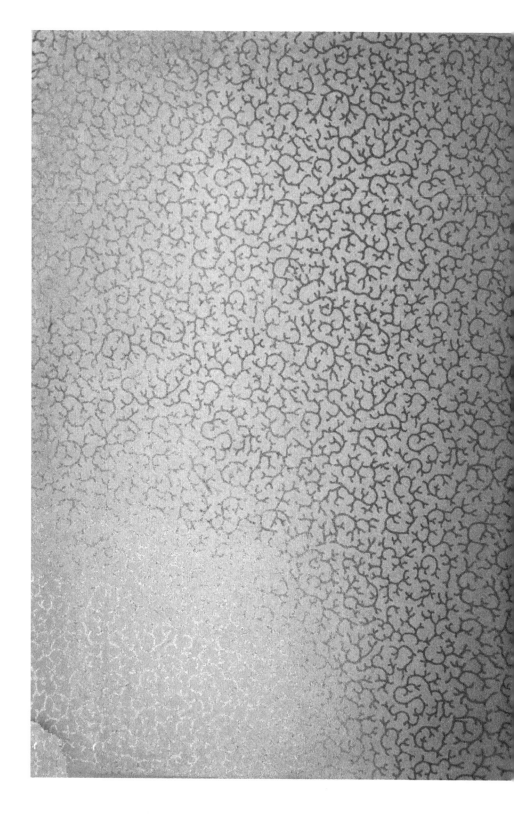

CPSIA information can be obtained
at www.ICGtesting.com
Printed in the USA
LVHW081107130721
692572LV00017B/182